Sketches From Concord And Appledore

by
Frank Preston Stearns

Sketches From Concord And Appledore
by Frank Preston Stearns

Copyright © 2023

All Rights reserved.

No part of this publication may be reproduced, stored in a retrieval system, or transmitted in any form or by any means, electronic, mechanical, photocopying or Otherwise, without the written permission of the publisher.
The author/editor asserts the moral right to be identified as the author/editor of this work.

ISBN: 978-93-60467-68-5

Published by

DOUBLE 9 BOOKS

2/13-B, Ansari Road
Daryaganj, New Delhi – 110002
info@double9books.com
www.double9books.com
Tel. 011-40042856

This book is under public domain

ABOUT THE AUTHOR

Frank Preston Stearns was a writer and abolitionist from Massachusetts in the 1800s. He was born in 1846 and died in 1917. His father was the abolitionist George Luther Stearns. He worked with Elizur Wright on ambitious anti-slavery projects like the American Anti-Slavery Society. He is also known for writing important books about the lives and careers of famous American authors and public figures, such as The Life and Genius of Nathaniel Hawthorne, The Life of Prince Otto von Bismarck, and The Life and Public Services of George Luther Stearns. The 4th of January 1846 saw the birth of Frank Preston Stearns in Medford, Massachusetts. On September 28, 1898, he married Emilia Maciel. They had one child after the wedding. He died in Arlington, Massachusetts, on January 21, 1917, from a brain bleed.

CONTENTS

PREFACE 7
CONCORD THIRTY YEARS AGO 8
HAWTHORNE 21
LOUISA M. ALCOTT 40
EMERSON HIMSELF 50
MATTHEW ARNOLD'S LECTURE 63
ARNOLD ON EMERSON 69
DAVID A. WASSON 72
WENDELL PHILLIPS 93
APPLEDORE AND THE LAIGHTONS 114
WHITTIER 129

PREFACE

A volume of reminiscences is commonly the last book that an author publishes, if indeed he does not leave the task to his literary administrator. There are not wanting, however, instances to the contrary; and in the present case my object is more especially to attract public attention to the lives and works of two distinguished men, one of whom has hitherto been little appreciated, and the other, as it seems to me, greatly misunderstood. My position in regard to David A. Wasson has already been challenged, but I have faith that it will endure the test of time. If these pages shall also succeed in restoring to Wendell Phillips a portion of the fame which he lost by the wayward course of his declining years, they will not have been written in vain. The other characters that I have brought upon this stage are such as both the writer and the public have long taken an interest in. To the few living personages who have been introduced, I would apologize, and excuse myself on the ground that the picture would be imperfect without them.

CONCORD THIRTY YEARS AGO

To one looking westward from Boston State House there appears a line of rugged, precipitous hills extending across the country from southwest to northeast. Having ascended these heights, we perceive beyond them an irregular line of pale blue mountains, of which Wachusett is the most southerly peak, and which is in fact a portion of the White Mountain range extending through New Hampshire and into the northern part of Maine. The watershed between these two forms the valley of the Concord and Merrimac Rivers, which is the first military line of defence in New England west of the sea-coast. It is for this reason that the first struggle for American independence took place on the banks of the Concord River, and not elsewhere; a fact that might have been predicted, though not of course with certainty, when Boston was first settled.

One would like to know how this rural community with martial destiny before it happened to obtain the name of Concord. Did the Rev. Peter Bulkley, descendant of the Plantagenets, who first organized society in that valley, did he come there for peace and repose after a religious controversy in Boston? No doubt the sloping hillsides and broad sunny plain with the sluggish river winding through it looked very restful to him, after the rugged country through which he had passed; but we fear that he found discord and contention already before him, as many have who came there since for a like purpose. Was there a strange fatality in the name, so that Patrick Henry might say with added force, "Gentlemen may cry peace, peace, but there is no peace"? Is it true that peace and war are reciprocal like night and day,—one a rest and preparation for the other, and at the same time its natural consequence? Certain it is that no individual life is interesting or valuable in which there has not been a severe struggle; and periods of warfare have often proved to be powerful stimulants for human energy and intellect. In one respect, however, the Rev. Peter Bulkley was fully justified, for Concord has become more famous in the arts of peace than if a Marengo or Gravelotte had been fought there. It has a place in the history of literature, and its name is pleasant either to speak or think of.

The town is beautifully situated and seems to sleep in the hollow of the hills. It is now a suburb of Boston, with artistic bridges, water from Sandy Pond, a bronze statue of the minute man, and a good deal of suburban elegance; but thirty years ago it was one of the neat, unpretending, yet so respectable looking, New England villages, such as are still to be met with in the central part of Massachusetts. The country roads wound into the town and wound out of it; the river crept lazily by with only a slight swirl or eddy on its surface; and the wild flowers on its banks bloomed and faded without attracting more attention than in the days of the Indians. Early in the morning ten or a dozen well-dressed gentlemen might be seen hastening to the railway station; then after the children had gone to school there was a nearly unbroken silence until they came out again. Occasionally a farmer in his hay-cart or other rude vehicle would jingle through the village, or a woman with a shawl and sun-bonnet would call at one of the stores, make some small purchase, and return as she came.

Towards evening the children would come out of school, and fill the streets with noise and excitement for a time; the gentlemen would return from Boston looking quite as much fatigued as if they had been working all day in a cornfield. The houses on Main Street were mostly so white as to be hardly distinguishable from the snow in winter, though many of them belonged, architecturally at least, to the last century, and had brass knockers on the doors. Yet there was a certain harmony among them; and it seemed as if the place must always have been as it was at that time.

There is, however, a compensation in the dullness of country life, which may be expressed in the word nature. The real architecture of Concord was not in private or public edifices, but in its magnificent elms, whose branches spanned the streets like the arches of a Gothic cathedral. The largest of them stands in front of the town hall, and its trunk measures just sixteen feet in circumference; though Doctor Holmes has failed to enumerate it in his list of the great trees of the State. Another on the road to Lexington is remarkable for its straight stem and perfect wineglass form. In autumn the scarlet maples set between the elms are no bad substitute for stained-glass windows.

There were no fine pictures in the town, but every turn of the river disclosed a landscape equal to a Claude or a Kenset. It is rare good fortune to live by a river of clear, pure water which serves equally well for boating and swimming or skating. There are very few such rivers. In the larger ones the current is usually too strong to make a long rowing expedition pleasant entertainment, and tide rivers are always inconvenient. In small rivers shoals and sand-bars commonly abound. River skating, also, is a science by itself, and requires, like Alpine climbing, well-seasoned knowledge and experience. It is a very different matter from whirling around in a city rink with half an inch of snow on the ice. The young men of Concord used to skate to Lowell, on favorable occasions, and back again, nearly thirty miles in all, and thought nothing of it. Concord River with its grassy banks, picturesque bridges and continual change of hill and meadow scenery is one of the prettiest that can be found anywhere.

Then such walks and drives as there were in the town! From Concord Common roads branch off in all directions like the spokes of a wheel. The oldest road, by which the British troops made their entry and exit, runs northeasterly to the Hawthorne house and Lexington with a firm, dry sidewalk for more than a mile; another goes northwesterly to the battleground and Esterbrook farm, where there were magnificent chestnut trees equal in size and shape to the Persian walnuts of Europe, as well as huge granite boulders scattered about from some pre-historic glacier.

The Emerson farm lies between two interesting roads, one going straight over the hills of Boston, and the other to Walden Lake and Thoreau's hermitage, or where it was. Between them runs a lively, gurgling brook, which used to be frequented by woodcock, and the Virginia rail, and passes close by Mrs. Emerson's garden.

Two or three miles to the south there is another lakelet called Fairhaven Bay, the south branch of the river flowing through it, quite equal in its way to Walden, or to an Irish lake, for that matter. On the outskirts of the village, there was many a quaint old weather-beaten house with a well-sweep, perhaps, for accompaniment, — excellent subjects for a sketchbook, — and Walden woods were always full of natural side-shows and those charming effects of color and shadow which artists delight in.

On the western side, there were the two mile square, the three mile square, and five mile square, for those who liked an exact measure for their constitutional exercise; and on the north the road went straight to Sleepy Hollow, now one of the famous cemeteries of the world. Thence, paths went through the fields and woods to the Lexington road on one side and to the north bridge on the other; and these paths are memorable from the fact that they were Hawthorne's favorite walk during the last years of his life.

A curious accident happened somewhere about 1860 just beyond Sleepy Hollow. A farmer returning to the next town felt the earth shaking under his wagon, and looked behind him just in time to see a piece of the road disappear into a pool of black water. The natives thought it had gone down to China for they were all summer filling the place up, and the expense was not less than that of a new district school-house.

The Indian name of the river was Muskataquid, and there was formerly an Indian encampment on the site of the old Ripley manse and battleground. A great quantity of arrow-heads of flint, jasper and quartz have been found in the neighboring fields, and Emerson used sometimes to bring his visitors to search for them. The Ripley family had a fine collection of Indian relics, and it is almost pathetic to think of the pains and labor the aborigines must have expended in manufacturing those household and warlike implements,—the arrows especially being often so soon lost again.

It is likely that they chose this situation for its sunny exposure, and as a favorable landing for their canoes, rather than from a decided feeling for landscape beauty. No doubt they had their battles and invasions, and perhaps repulsed their enemies from the same ground where the British line was afterwards formed.

What one wonders at, in regard to the Concord fight, is that the English commander should have drawn off his men after the first volley and so slight a loss. He had as good a position as his opponents, and after an obstinate struggle might have succeeded in carrying the bridge, the bayonets of his soldiers giving him a certain advantage. This would seem to have been more prudent than to retreat so long a distance before a confident enemy. It has been agreed that the position of the minute men was the best they could have selected, for after repulsing the British troops they were able to send a detachment across by Sleepy Hollow and Hawthorne's path to attack them again in flank on the Lexington road. This success was as fortunate for the colonies as in the summer of 1861 Bull Run was unlucky for our Southern friends.

The men who were drawn up to be shot at on Lexington Common were no doubt as brave as their friends who contested the battle of the old north bridge, but their position was not a favorable one to hold against a superior force. It was an excellent position to retreat from, and perhaps that is what their commander had in view. Evidently they should have withdrawn to Concord, or have intrenched themselves on the nearest hillside commanding the Boston and Concord road. Such was the difference between these two fights.

The life of Concord, at the time of which we write, was not its celebrated people so much as Mr. Frank B. Sanborn's school for youth of both sexes. There were not young people enough in the town to make a dance or a picnic out of, and this school introduced an element from the outside world which was both useful and improving. Most of his pupils came from the vicinity of Boston, but there were many also from Springfield, now and then one from the West Indies, and finally a Sandwich Islander, a genuine Kanaka. They supported several boarding-houses, the candy-store and the corner grocery, besides greatly increasing the revenue of the post-office.

It was a cheerful sight to see these ruddy youths and blooming maidens of a winter's day come trooping in to get the evening mail with their skates in their hands. There was also a daily delegation of farmers' boys from Acton, staunch, worthy fellows, and generally better behaved than their more aristocratic companions.

Mr. Sanborn himself, (afterwards for more than twenty years the efficient inspector of our state charities,) was the most genial and good-humored of schoolmasters. He enjoyed teaching, and wished his scholars to enjoy learning. He liked to see the bright young faces about him, and it was their own fault if he was not liked by his pupils. He was impartial, frank, and perfectly sincere; knew how to keep discipline without being a martinet. He was especially a good instructor for young ladies for he never showed them any sentimental tenderness.

It was not a very good training school, like the Boston Latin School, or Phillips Academy at Exeter, and this is usually the case in a school where there are pretty young women; but, as Emerson indeed said, much could be learned with Mr. Sanborn which was not to be had at other schools,— especially this, that the true aim of life should not be riches or success or even scholarship, but moral and intellectual development. Mr. Sanborn's ideal of his profession was a high one, and but for his interest in the larger field of philanthropy he might have succeeded in realizing it.

Mr. Sanborn's most troublesome boy had a scriptural name, which we will call David,—afterwards quite a distinguished lawyer. There was no harm in David, but an immense deal of mischief. In fact he was irrepressible. "David, stand up on the floor," was part of the customary routine; and when this was accompanied by the use of a large lexicon his situation was a truly amusing one. If he succeeded in escaping this penalty of transgression until the first recess he was considered fortunate. He usually returned from the school sports too much exhausted for any further exertion, but in half an hour was as lively again as ever. All veneration for authority seemed to have been replaced in David by a strong sense of the ridiculous. His seat was immediately under the eye of the master, with his face to the wall, and a large map of ancient Rome before him, but this did not prevent him from turning about on all possible occasions and expressing his various states of mind in such ludicrous pantomime as would set off the young girls and small boys like a row of torpedoes. Whatever might be said or done in the school without bringing condign punishment on his head David was sure to say or do; and his criticism of passing events and comments during recitations were quite as edifying as those of the instructor,—which is saying a good deal. He had committed to memory one of the longest lists of exceptions in the Latin grammar, and never missed an opportunity of repeating it as rapidly as possible and with a comical look.

His one object of aversion was Mr. Sanborn's rattan, and what to do about it he did not know; until coming to school one morning very early with another youth of the same disposition, they cut it into sections and smoked it. After this he was in great terror for several days lest the theft should be discovered, but as the rattan was more for ornament than exercise, its absence did not appear to have been noticed. Of course these performances made quite a hero of him with the girls, and he was rewarded with their smiles and favor at the school dances and other social occasions.

As an artistic contrast to this picture we remember three beautiful girls who boarded with the wife of the village blacksmith, in one of the whitest and most neatly kept houses in the town. They were not merely pretty young women, but each possessed a style of beauty peculiarly her own. One was a bright, rosy blonde, with sparkling eyes and a lively, spirited manner; another more quiet and composed, with an ivory-white complexion, and large, dreamy, tender-looking eyes; and the third was a light brunette with an oval face and regular features, reserved and dignified. Slightly idealized, with these fine qualities, they might have served for a picture of the Three Graces. They had the advantage of pretty manners, and being fast friends and of a single mind, made a strong impression wherever they went. Though the eldest was not more than seventeen, the Bigelow girls, as they were called from the blacksmith's family name, took the lead in Concord social life for the time being, and gave a tone to it. Their influence helped to make the boys more manly and the other girls more respectful.

Such a trio could not long escape the notice of the Harvard students, a number of whom made their acquaintance through graduates of the school; and one of them, inspired with admiration, composed a song which was quite popular at the time, beginning thus:

"There was an old lady in Concord did dwell,
Who had but three boarders, and each one a belle;
Grace, Jennie and Maggie, more priceless than pearls;
Then here's to the health of the Bigelow girls."

Truly the days of their youth were the days of their glory; but it is not so for everyone. In fact many of us never obtain any glory. And who is that plainly dressed girl with the meekly determined look who goes back and forth so quietly and regularly? If you speak to her she will smile, but her voice is not often heard. It is Miss Evans' Mary Garth, or the prototype of Louisa Alcott's "Old Fashioned Girl." She is the best scholar in school, and already has important plans in her mind for the future.

Mr. Alcott would sometimes come in on a Wednesday afternoon, listen to the declamations and afterwards give his young friends a conversation on the faculties of the human mind. He was an agreeable speaker, and knew how to hold the attention of his youthful audience. On one of these occasions while he was discoursing on the higher mental faculties which are not possessed by the lower animals, a small boy suddenly called out from his corner, "Dogs have a conscience; I've seen it." The whole school roared at this, and it nearly disconcerted Mr. Alcott; but he quickly recovered himself, and explained that the apprehension of punishment often supplies the place of a conscience in dogs, as well as in boys and men; and a highly interesting discussion ensued on this subject. Such a method of instruction was highly refreshing after the dry routine in Latin and mathematics.

There was a yearly nutting excursion in October to Esterbrook farm where there were tall chestnut trees, flying squirrels and plenty of wood for a bonfire. May-day was usually celebrated at Conantum,—a pine-clad hill on the south side of Fairhaven Bay, opposite the cliffs. As soon as winter came committees were chosen to provide dancing or theatricals for every Friday evening; but the climax of pleasure was a half-holiday for a skating carnival on Walden Pond,—where Thoreau was sure to be present, and also a Miss Caroline Moore, daughter of the deputy sheriff, and afterwards widely known in Europe and America as the skatorial queen.

"Three cheers for the Giver of this glorious afternoon," and then the caps would go up in the air, and the rocks and hills echo the hoarse shouts of the boys. I can hear now the jingling of the skates, the crackling of the snow and the merry laughter as we came from under the pine trees of Walden into the keen starlight, with the great comet streaming in front of us.

On the first of May, 1859, Emerson wrote in a letter to Carlyle: "My boy divides his time between Cicero and cricket,—and will go to college next year. Sam Ward and I tickled each other the other day, in looking over a very good company of young people, by finding in the newcomers a marked improvement on their parents."

There are those who still remember seeing the two distinguished men on the Concord playground, and wondering what they thought of it. Mr. Ward came to place his boy under Mr. Sanborn's care; and a remarkable boy he proved to be,—equally generous, fearless and high-minded. Twenty years later, that same boy, looking out of his New York office window, saw his former guide and preceptor striding through Wall Street. He rushed down the stairs, and out upon the sidewalk, but the friend of his youth had disappeared and was nowhere to be found.

With two or three exceptions, Mr. Sanborn's young men held him in high regard, and when, in 1860, the United States marshals tried to carry him off by force to testify at Washington in regard to the Harper's Ferry invasion, they all rushed to his rescue, and foremost among them a Baltimore boy, who had been cursing his teacher as an infernal abolitionist for the previous six months.

Mr. Sanborn is much better known for his connection with the Harper's Ferry invasion than for his Concord school, or later service on the board of State Charities. He was secretary of the Kansas Aid Committee in Boston during 1856, and in this way became acquainted with John Brown, who visited the school, and the two were afterwards intimate friends.

None of Brown's New England supporters approved of his invasion of Virginia, and Mr. Sanborn especially argued the matter with him and endeavored to dissuade him from it. He thus became acquainted, however, with Brown's plans, and was the only person outside of Brown's immediate followers who knew of the proposed attack on Harper's Ferry. When the attempt failed and John Brown was a prisoner in Charlestown jail, Mr. Sanborn found himself, as an accessory before the act, in a most trying situation. If carried to Virginia either as a witness or as "particeps criminis" his chance for life would be a slight one. The question was, would General Banks, who was then governor of Massachusetts, refuse to surrender him. John A. Andrew did not consider it safe to rely on him; and Mr. Sanborn accordingly disappeared for the winter, his school being carried on meanwhile by an assistant and some public spirited Concord ladies, one of whom was a sister of Hon. E. R. Hoar.

In the spring Mr. Sanborn reappeared, and was almost immediately summoned by a United States marshal to give an account of himself before the senate committee in Washington. This he declined to do, believing that the townspeople would forcibly resist any attempts to carry him off.

The marshal, however, set a trap for him that missed little of being successful. He came to Concord at midnight, and secreted himself in an old barn which was close to the school-house, and belonged to one Mr. Holbrook, a custom-house officer. There he remained all the next day, keeping watch of Mr. Sanborn's movements through the cracks in the boards. A little after nine in the evening he was joined by four assistants in a carriage. They then proceeded to Mr. Sanborn's house, seized him at the door, and in spite of his great size and strength, would certainly have carried him off had it not been for the courage and energy of his sister Sarah. She screamed "murder," and seizing the carriage-whip, made such good use of it that the horses were with difficulty prevented from running away.

Her cries waked up the blacksmith in the next house, and he quickly came to the rescue. The "Bigelow girls" ran through the village like wild cats ringing door-bells and calling on the people. In less than twenty minutes nearly every man in town, Emerson included, was on the spot. The crowd showed a determined spirit, and the marshals were probably glad enough when Judge Hoar appeared with a writ of "habeas corpus," and took the prisoner out of their hands in a legal manner. The case was tried in Boston next day, and Mr. Sanborn was adjudged to have the right of it. A lively celebration followed in the Concord town hall that evening, and Miss Sarah Sanborn was presented with an elegant revolver; but the old borough had not been so stirred up since '75.

The place was not without some small entertainments. Every autumn there was an annual cattle-show at which the same bulls, horses and poultry were brought for exhibition, and one might suppose also the same fruit and vegetables; for they differed little in appearance from one year to another. A live bittern in a cage of laths was an unusual curiosity. Ventriloquists and every kind of a juggler, as well as native Indians and the wild men of Borneo, came to perform in the town hall.

Then there was the Concord Lyceum. People in those days believed in obtaining nourishment for the mind as well as the body. Pretty dry nourishment it often proved to be; but it served to bring them together for an hour or two, and take them out of themselves and their dull routine. Wiser remarks and more fresh information were sometimes heard upon the stairway than in the lecture-hall.

Yet Emerson was always good, and every man and woman who came to hear him probably felt better for it, even if they were unable to comprehend what he said to them. In the mind's eyes one can see now his spare figure standing at the desk between two large kerosene lamps, bending forward slightly to catch the familiar sentence with his eye, and then calmly surveying his audience as if to see where he could deliver it most effectively.

Henry Ward Beecher drew the largest house, and produced great enthusiasm by comparing the United States to an elephant,—though at that time there can hardly be said to have been any United States; but the fine oratory of Wendell Phillips made the strongest impression, rather too rhetorical to be permanent—but it was intense while it lasted. A young lady who was obliged to take laughing-gas a few days after his lecture on Toussaint L'Ouverture repeated passages from it with appropriate gestures, in the dentist's chair, and finally concluded, not with the name of the negro statesman, but of the Concord high-school teacher. Phillips was an especial favorite with the older ladies of the town, who organized a local anti-slavery society in his honor, and held a meeting of it whenever he came there.

But neither Phillips nor Beecher could equal a lecture by the Unitarian clergyman on the naval policy of England, which was based on valuable facts and might well be compared to a few grains of wheat in the midst of infinite chaff.

Judge Hoar did not lecture before the lyceum, which seemed strange, for he was not only a man of vigorous intellect, but had, as Lowell said,

"More wit and gumption and shrewd Yankee sense
Than there are mosses on an old stone-fence,"

and he could have made any subject interesting in which he was interested himself.

The Hoar family for some time past had been almost kings in Concord, as frequently happens where there is an uncommonly strong man, either a lawyer or a manufacturer, in a town of two or three thousand inhabitants. They were a hardy New England race, lawyers by an inherited tendency, and had now made their mark in public affairs for three generations. They can count among their immediate relatives more senators and representatives to Congress than any other American family. It was said in 1775 that while Samuel Adams represented the force and virtue of New England life, John Adams was the best product of its cultivated side; and it would seem as if old Samuel Hoar, the founder of his line, were a mean between the two. Fortunate is such a father if he has a son who inherits his talents and virtues as well as his property; and fortunate is the son whose father knows from his own experience what is best to do for him.

The Judge was always an interesting figure in the Concord streets, and also a pleasant person to meet, for there was never the least pretention about him. He usually had the air of a man with an object before him, and yet it was sufficiently evident that he did not intend to claim more than his rightful share. He walked the ground with a tenacious step, but with no unseemly haste. There was a keen, frosty sparkle in his eye, and a certain severity of manner which, however, covered a great deal of kindness. He liked successful men such as were his own equal in ability, but he was quite as likely to take an interest in those who were unfortunate. A brother of Dr. Holmes, a constant invalid and great sufferer, who required much consideration, was a more frequent visitor at his house than Lowell or Agassiz. His face bore a striking resemblance to Raphael's portrait of the war-like Pope Julius Second, the last of the great popes. He admired Emerson, and was frequently seen in his company; but Alcott and Thoreau he seemed to have little respect for. Mr. Alcott once said, "I suppose Judge Hoar looks on me as the most useless person on the continent; but I can at least appreciate *him*."

He was the youngest judge that had ever been appointed to the supreme bench of Massachusetts, member of Congress, president of the Harvard

Alumni, etc.; but his real distinction now is that as a member of General Grant's cabinet he was the first American in public life to take a determined stand in regard to civil-service reform.

For thirty years he had seen the government patronage turned into an enormous engine of political corruption, and endure it longer he could not. He went to Washington, much to his own inconvenience, mainly to strike a blow at this monster. Did he realize the magnitude of the work before him—one which thousands of patriotic men have since attempted and signally failed to accomplish? It was like taking the meat away from a tiger, or trying to lift the Mitgard serpent. Judge Hoar found himself quite alone in the president's cabinet, and with the exception of Sumner, Garfield, and a few others, senators and representatives united against him in a massive phalanx. Even the friendship of General Grant was unable to protect him from the fury of his opponents. He returned, not unwillingly, to his native heath and the practice of a better profession than Washington politics.

In his report to Congress on the battle of Bull Run, General Winfield Scott gave the opinion that it was lost through the lack of capable officers for the volunteer regiments; and it is generally true that men who like to play soldier in time of peace are not the best material to make real soldiers out of. This would not apply however to Captain George L. Prescott of Concord, who commanded the embattled farmers in that engagement. He was leading an advance on the enemy's centre—"a magnificent sight to look at," his colonel said—when the right wing of the army was outflanked by General Kirby Smith, and the Union forces obliged to retreat. The colonel also appears to have done his duty there, and being severely wounded at this juncture could hear nothing in the feverish condition he was in for the next few days but Prescott saying, "Steady, men, steady!" to the soldiers. Previous to 1861 he was station master at Concord, and also carried on a business in lumber, cement, and other building materials, which he could easily do, for trains in those days were not so very numerous. He was the first person that attracted the attention of visitors to the town; for he had a commanding figure and a frank, manly countenance, only too fearless and kindly,—a very handsome man. The Hoar family were evidently Yankees, and so were Emerson, Alcott, and Sanborn, but Captain Prescott was an American without seeming to belong to any particular part of the country. His cordial frankness and independence of manner reminded one of a Virginian.

The refined side of his nature is indicated by an anecdote of his first few days in camp on the Potomac. A cadet freshly graduated from West Point was directed by General McDowell to drill the different companies of the regiment in succession, and having but slight respect for volunteer soldiers, he gave an emphasis to his orders by the plentiful use of profane language. When he came to the Concord company, Captain Prescott, who was standing at one side, walked across to him and said, "I must request you, Sir, to give your orders in the plain terms of the military code, for my men do not like profanity. If you do otherwise, I shall order them to march off the ground; and they will obey me and not you." This brought the cadet to terms very quickly.

In the spring of 1862 he recruited another company for the Massachusetts Thirty-second; soon rose to the rank of colonel; and after escaping the peril of a dozen hard-fought battles, he was finally killed, with nearly half his command, in Grant's advance upon Richmond. Perhaps no other man would have been so greatly missed in his native town.

Thoreau used to walk through Concord with the long step of an Indian, looking straight before him, but at the same time observing everything. Occasionally he would stop, make an incision in the bark of a tree with his knife, or pick up a stone and examine it. It was not often that he was met with in anybody's house, or seen in company with other men.

His profession was that of a surveyor; and it is easy to imagine how, with his poetic temperament, while laying out roads and measuring wood-lots, he came to be what he was. Many people thought his peculiar ways were an affectation, but I believe that he was one of the plainest and simplest of men; as plain and single-minded as President Lincoln himself. It was his theory of the way men should live. He was a Diogenes without being a cynic.

James Russell Lowell (as he himself tells us) was sent to Concord to rusticate while he was at college, and conceived at that time an aversion for Thoreau which never left him. In his celebrated "Fable for Critics" he satirized him as an imitator of Emerson, and so plainly that there was no mistaking the portrait. This could not have troubled Thoreau much for he was a perfect stoic, and cared little for the opinions of others so long as he satisfied his own conscience. Emerson, however, felt it keenly, for it was equally a reflection on his friend and his own sagacity. In his last volume of poems Lowell also speaks of Emerson in a way which indicates rather a diminished respect for him.

It is true that Thoreau imitated Emerson's manner of speech a good deal—and it was often difficult to avoid doing this while in Emerson's company—but Lowell also in his younger days affected a grave and reserved demeanor which he afterwards became tired of and threw entirely aside. About the time of which we speak Emerson complained that he saw too little of Thoreau, and was afraid that he avoided him. The man was sufficiently original. He did not pretend to be a poet, and his prose writing is not at all like Emerson. In point of style it is purer and more classic than either Emerson's or Lowell's; and these two lines of his,

"In the good then who can trust.
Only the wise are just,"

certainly deserve to be set up somewhere in letters of gold.

He had a strong dislike of matrimony. Once while walking across a field with David A. Wasson he kicked a skunk-cabbage with his boot and said, "There, marriage is like that." Lowell was without doubt right about him in this respect. Thoreau's notions of life, like the socialistic theories of Henry George, would if generally adopted put an end to civilization. He wanted like the French theorists of the last century to separate himself from the history of his race; a most dangerous attempt. It is like cutting a tree from its roots. Wasson had many a hard argument with him on this point, and tried to show him that customs are the good logic of the human race: but it was too late. However, logic is one thing and character another.

The best eulogy of Thoreau is to be found in Emerson's poetry. He is evidently the subject of the beautiful little poem called "Forbearance." The opening lines,

"Thou who hast named the birds without a gun;
Loved the wood-rose, and left it on its stalk;
At rich men's tables eaten bread and pulse;—"

This describes the hermit of blue Walden exactly. A large portion of "Woodnotes" is devoted to an account of his pilgrimage in the forests of Maine; and the ode to "Friendship" must have been inspired either by him or Carlyle.

"I fancied he was fled—
And after many a year,
Glowed unexhausted kindliness,
Like daily sunrise there."

He delivered a lecture one winter before the Concord lyceum on wild apple-trees. The subject made his audience laugh, but their laughter was of short duration. The man who had lived there so long unknown was at last revealed before them, It was the best lecture of the season, and at its close there was long continued applause.

HAWTHORNE

The literary celebrities of Concord, with the exception of Thoreau, were not indigenous. Emerson may have gone there from an hereditary tendency, but more likely because his cousins the Ripleys dwelt there. Hawthorne came there by way of the Brook Farm experiment. How, with his reserved and solitary mode of life, he should have embarked in such a gregarious enterprise is not very clear; but the election of General Harrison had deprived him of a small government office—it seems as if Webster might have interfered in his behalf—his writings brought him very little, and perhaps he hardly knew what to do with himself.

All accounts agree that he joined the West Roxbury association of his own free-will, and without solicitation of any kind. He not only threw himself into this hazardous scheme with an energy that astounded his friends but he embarked in it all the money he had in the world, which was nearly a thousand dollars. He has left no explanation from which we might infer what his hopes or his motives were.

Since three wise men went to sea in a bowl, or the army of German children set out for the Holy Land in the twelfth century, there was never a more hare-brained or chimerical undertaking. I once knew of a boy who after much reading of Robinson Crusoe, started for the woods at five o'clock of a summer afternoon, with the full intention of spending the night there alone. He took with him a light fowling-piece, and some crackers in his jacket pocket. He gathered some berries and shot some small birds, and cooked them after the Indian fashion. When it grew dark, however, he became frightened and climbed into a tree; but he could not sleep there, and finally returned home about one o'clock in the morning to find his family in great agitation.

This was not very unlike the Brook Farm enterprise, which was inspired by the writings of Fourier, a seductive French socialist and one of the most unreasonable of men. He considered, like Diogenes, that since all men could not be rich and comfortable, it was better that they should all be needy and miserable. It was one of the sentimental out-growths of the French Revolution, for which Napoleonism is always the proper remedy. One of his peculiar notions was that every man should black his own boots.

George Ripley and his friends do not seem to have made any definite calculation of what might be the result of their experiment. They expected, by working six hours a day and limiting themselves to the simplest and most frugal living, to have six left for literary pursuits and the enjoyment of profound conversation. Any practical farmer would have told them that this could not be done and make both ends meet at the close of the year. Any political economist would have told them that a community which disregards the advantage of division of labor, could not compete with one which recognizes that advantage. The principles of Fourier, if generally adopted, would produce general starvation and soon reduce the population of Europe to one fourth of its present numbers. London, which depends for its size on its commercial and political importance, would become almost as desolate as ancient Thebes.

There was lately an essay published in one of our magazines entitled, "Why Socialism appeals to Artists," and the reason alleged was that artists, being more sensitive and delicately organized than most people, were less capable of enduring the hard struggle with the world which all are obliged to sustain who make their own way in it. This is no doubt the true explanation of the Brook Farm enterprise, and it carries with it its own contradiction. The more realistic sort of literature might survive in the communistic order, but sculpture and painting, which depend upon the undivided surplus of production which we call wealth, would inevitably perish. Even literature would disappear at length, then science, or at least all advancement of science, precedent in law would be disregarded, and the dark ages come again. The present organization of society is the accumulated wisdom of mankind for thousands of years. Like the language we speak, it was rather an intellectual growth than the invention of an individual or any number of individuals. Those who have done the most for it have added but little to the whole. It may be subverted by revolution for a time, but will always reassert itself again. It may be amended or modified by reason, but cannot be replaced, either by the ingenuity of one man or that of a whole generation.

The logic of custom is the most cogent of all reasoning, for it is inherited in our veins from our ancestors. The man who tries to escape from it is like a plant being pulled up by the roots. It is exactly this which writers like Fourier and Henry George leave out of their reckoning. They see that in individual cases custom is often blind, cruel, and oppressive, and being kind-hearted and sympathetic they hate it; but they might as well hate the earth itself because there are deserts and swamps and malarious places on its surface. It is, no doubt, the special business of man to remodel the earth as much as possible; to drain its swamps, and level its forests; but in spite of that its rivers and mountains will always remain the same, and separate ourselves from it we cannot.

The greater number of the Brook Farm community were transcendentalists, and we have no desire to depreciate the work which the transcendentalists accomplished. They were the needful men and women of their time; the importers of fresh thought and a more elevated mental activity. The most critical and conservative of American reviews has said of them:

"They put aside worldly ambition and desire as truly as ever did medieval monk or oriental ascetic, and thus gave what was essential in their surroundings, a practical proof of their sincerity. The result was almost startling. Their Yankee audience first ridiculed them as dreamers; but when they found that what the transcendentalists actually recommended to them was dreaming, their ridicule changed to wonder, and finally to a sort of awe-struck admiration, something like that we imagine a Roman to have felt on learning that a Christian was capable of giving up his fish-ponds and nightingales' tongues, and his afternoons at the amphitheatre, for the sake of what he called 'Truth' proclaimed by an obscure few."

This is not saying too much, but if anything too little. Since the time of the early Christians there was never a more pure-minded and loyal-hearted congregation than that which was gathered at Brook Farm. They were really the best society of the day. George Ripley himself, one of the finest scholars and most agreeable writers of that time, afterwards found his right place as literary editor of the New York Tribune, where for twenty-five years he disseminated the knowledge of the best thought and literature broadcast over the land. When we consider the immense circulation of that periodical and the quality of its readers, we can hardly overestimate the value of his work. Many have become famous for less.

There were poets, painters, musicians in the community; especially John S. Dwight, who as the life-long editor of the "Journal of Music," also deserves a place on the roll of our public educators. George William Curtis was one of the youngest members of the community, but always one of the most brilliant. Sometimes of a rainy day there was very good cheer and entertainment in the "Hive" as they called their most commodious building, but generally the men were too drowsy and fatigued after their work was done for much intellectual activity.

It is necessary, however, to distinguish between the New England transcendentalists and the German school of philosophy, from which they are supposed to have derived their inspiration. A German critic has said of them that they were not so much philosophers as poetical rhapsodists, and this is about the truth of it. Their business was not so much thinking, as to celebrate thinking. There was also in the composition of their creed a strong element of French naturalism, which is not easily reconciled with the teachings of the German transcendentalists. Kant, Fichte, and Schelling were true metaphysicians, and would never have encouraged their pupils to establish a socialistic community in the suburbs of Leipsic, nor would they have approved of Emerson's lines:

"Who liveth with the stalwart pine
Foundeth an heroic line;
Who liveth in the palace hall
Waneth fast and spendeth all;—"

for they would have said, "There are the Hohenzollerns; and the experience of mankind is also worth something." It was this empirical French quality in New England transcendentalism which gave it a certain popularity, but at the same time prevented it from striking its roots deeply into the national soil. The law of nature has its value, but where it conflicts with the historical method it is invariably defeated.

Emerson was the elected chief of the transcendental movement on account of his influence with the public, but its true leader and representative character was Margaret Fuller.

This remarkable woman, whose life was adventure from the cradle, who lived in everybody's house except her own, who went everywhere and did everything on nothing a year, who made enemies by the dozen and friends by the score, still remains one of the most distinguished persons of that period. With some faults of character, she still possessed those strong qualities which are required for the conduct of a great enterprise. She had that personal magnetism which comes from courage, confidence, and clear perceptions. She inspired great enthusiasm in others for whatever she was interested in herself.

As a talker, she was the rival of Carlyle and Coleridge; the best we have ever had on this side of the water, and with such an artistic style that one could hardly decide whether it was studied or natural. She was a terrible antagonist; for she united the tongue of a woman to the logical faculty of a man, and it was impossible to get the better of her. Her faults were the faults of youth, as she was occasionally vain, saucy or overbearing, and always self-conscious. It was this last trait that Lowell referred to when he represented her as saying that since her earliest years she had "lived cheek by jowl with the Infinite Soul." Much youthful vanity, however, can be forgiven to those who are generous and faithful. Besides, Margaret Fuller was splendidly domestic. She advocated women's rights to a certain extent;

but she was no forerunner to the modern brood of platform women who fumble their night-keys while they discourse on the duties of wives and mothers. She carried a helping hand into the families that she entered, as well as stirring all the inmates to an unwonted mental activity. She would knit socks while she talked Plato: but the best testimony to her character is the character of her friends. People are known by the company they keep.

The one quality which Hawthorne had in common with the transcendentalists, except such qualities as are common to all good people, was ideality. Next to the grand structure of his head, this is the most noticeable characteristic in the pictures of him. He seems to have been attracted to them at first, and was even mistaken for a transcendentalist by Edgar A. Poe, and was attacked by that fiery Virginian in a most belligerent manner.

At Brook Farm, however, he soon began to differentiate from them, and finally acquired for them something like an aversion. Neither is this to be wondered at. Hawthorne was an artist pure and simple. He looked for ideality in human life; not in the ideas that control and direct it. He was not like Raphael and Shakspeare, men who could enjoy philosophy and make their art so much the richer and deeper for it. He saw everything in a pictorial form; facts and conditions which did not make a picture had no value for him, and reasoning was a weariness and a disagreeable effort. Nevertheless he did the best he could.

It is delightful to think of the tremendous energy with which he worked at Brook Farm. No one else seems to have done so much hard labor there. He was better fitted for this than many of his colleagues, having a strong, full-chested frame, and is said in his youth to have been a very swift runner and skater; but nothing indicates better the latent force that was in this quiet and usually inactive man. Many of the Brook Farm adventurers were not physically equal to a solid day's work, but this was a contingency which nobody had foreseen.

Hawthorne was one of the first to discover the futility of the experiment. Early in the following year he wrote to Miss Sophia Peabody to whom he was then engaged: "It has become quite evident to me that our fortunes are not to be found in this place;" a conclusion which he no doubt arrived at from an examination of the accounts of the association. It was Hawthorne's salvation in the difficult path of life he had chosen; a path as difficult and dangerous as that of an Alpine climber, that, poet as he was, he always looked facts sternly in the face and did not permit himself to be misled by romantic or sentimental illusions.

It had been expected that the more brilliant members of the community would be able to write magazine articles, or other remunerative literature, in their hours of leisure, and money thus obtained would go into the common fund. Hawthorne found that he could do nothing of the kind. Two or three hours' work in the sun did not quite deprive him of the use of his brains, but it left him without either fancy or imagination. He also felt the want of that external refinement which a nature like Hawthorne's requires as a fulfilment of its internal condition. The lack of nicety in the housekeeping became continually more and more unpleasant to him. The expenditures at the end of the first year were largely in excess of the receipts; in fact the inmates had eaten up nearly everything that the farm produced. His friend Franklin Pierce, who was just beginning to be prominent in politics, asked him the salutary question, "What are you gaining by this peculiar mode of life?"

His experience there served as a foundation for the "Blithedale Romance," and caused no further injury than the loss of his money. It would have required a Thackeray to have realized and described the humorous side of it—the highly practical joke of so many well-educated and cultivated people making life unnecessarily hard for themselves.

In the autumn of 1841 a reverend gentleman, the brother of Mrs. L. Maria Child, went to visit his friend at Brook Farm accompanied by his niece, who is one of the few persons now living who have a distinct memory of the place. On calling at the "Hive" they learned that only a few members of the association were present at that moment, but Mr. Ripley himself could be found in the turnip field, where they soon discovered him with two others, throwing turnips into a cart. On the approach of his friends, Mr. Ripley came forward and said, "Dr. Francis, this is really kind of you, to come such a distance to see an old fellow. You perceive I am occupied with the philosophy of 'de cart.'" This referred to some writings he had lately published on Descartes' philosophy, and made his audience laugh heartily.

Mr. Dwight then appeared and gave an interesting account of a flock of wild geese which he had discovered early in the morning marching through the cornfield. He said they looked exactly like tame geese, but as soon as he came in sight of them they flew away in a most surprising manner. Mr. Bradford, who is frequently mentioned in Hawthorne's note-book, looked sunburnt and very thin, and averred that milking the cows on a frosty morning was a chilly kind of business. Hawthorne himself had gone to Boston; probably to sell the pig referred to in his conversation with Franklin Pierce. The visitors walked about the premises and were shown through the "Hive," but found it rather a dreary and comfortless building. The farm did not appear to be well kept. There was too evidently a lack of order and discipline there; and without order and discipline no enterprise in which numbers are concerned can succeed.

Having discovered nothing better than fool's gold at Brook Farm, Hawthorne suddenly came across the true metal in the domestic privacy of his married life at Concord. It would appear from one of Mrs. Hawthorne's letters that George Ripley was so sanguine of the success of his experiment that he had given Hawthorne a sort of guarantee for the thousand dollars which the latter had invested in it. When, at the close of the first year, Hawthorne had decided to withdraw from the association, he naturally hoped to regain a portion of his capital. Mr. Ripley was too deeply involved to accommodate him in that way, and offered instead the rent of the old Ripley mansion in Concord, which then happened to be vacant. So Hawthorne and Miss Peabody were happily married, with no immediate fund save the rent of an ancient house in the country, and no better expectations than the uncertain income from his pen.

It was a hazardous undertaking, but he was now nearly forty years old, his *fiancee* more than thirty, nor could the sharpest foresight discover any advantage from waiting longer. Emerson, in his lecture on heroism, has signalled especially the heroism of the scholar, and selected as an example the Frenchman Anquetil Duperron, who worked his passage on a vessel to India, and then worked his way, mostly on foot, through Afghanistan and Persia, learning languages as he went, in order to obtain copies of the sacred books of the Persians, which were then unknown in Europe. Were it not for fear of giving offence he might have found a finer heroism in literary genius, and selected an example from his own village.

For fifteen years Hawthorne had been like a ship detained from port by adverse winds. The handsomest and most gifted man in America had nearly reached to forty years without being married or finding a home of his own. It was a life of hardship; of social starvation almost like exile. It tested his courage, his faith in human nature, to the utmost. How difficult were the earlier years of Irving and Bryant and Longfellow. That he remained always true to himself and never lost sight of that ideal of excellence which was his guiding-star.

We are not surprised to learn that his difficulties were rather augmented than diminished by matrimony. Even in plain, rural Concord he found at the end of three years, that his expenses had exceeded his income by what seemed to him quite a formidable debt. This distressed him the more because he had not yet learned that all men must lose in some manner, and that the whole community is bound to take a share in such losses as are honestly incurred. This is what charity and philanthropy, as well as the various forms of insurance, finally result in. But Hawthorne was the last man to apply such a principle to his own case. He had continually hoped that when a balance-sheet was drawn up at Brook Farm some portion of his investment there would be returned to him; but this resource also failed him.

At last Bancroft the historian, whom James K. Polk strangely enough had made secretary of the navy, heard of his situation, and had him appointed collector of the port at Salem. He was again removed from that position by President Taylor, and it has been said that his wife heroically supported him by her skill in drawing and painting until the "Scarlet Letter" could be finished and money procured from its publication. The nomination of Franklin Pierce for the presidency was a piece of good fortune for Hawthorne such as the wildest expectation could never have imagined; and at length in his fiftieth year, with the consulate of Liverpool, he finally saw the wolves driven from his door. This realistic side of his life seems to have escaped the attention of his biographers.

Yet he may be called fortunate to have lived when he did. It is easy to say that we should have appreciated Emerson and Hawthorne better than their cotemporaries appreciated them, but it is one thing to recognize a genius when we meet him and a very different matter to admire him after we have been informed that he is a famous man. It is doubtful if writers in whom the ideality is so strongly marked would be received with favor at the present time either by editors or the public. The tendency to materialism would have been too strong for them. Lyceum lectures, on which Emerson depended chiefly, are not what they were; and either of them in a magazine would appear in too startling a contrast with the smooth impersonal writing of to-day. The two cardinal sins of a writer now are to have a style of his own and ideas of his own.

Complaint is frequently made that we have no great men like those of the past; but such grand individualities as Hawthorne and Webster, or even self-centred characters like Horace Greeley, are no longer possible. Everywhere, in the college, in the market, and in society, war is waged upon originality and independence of character. It is the same in politics as in literature. Our novelist critic said of the rage for Christmas cards, some years since, "The truth is that art must obey the popular will or cease to be." There was not much art certainly in Christmas cards; but nothing could express better the truculent spirit of the age.

Most husbands are fortunate if their honeymoon lasts a month, but Hawthorne's lasted two years. It would seem as if during that space not a cloud came across his sky. He gathered flowers for his wife—water lilies, which he must have sought for in a boat, fringed gentians and the queenly "Lilium Canadensis"—and then felt that the most beautiful of them were unequal to the loveliness of her nature. After the first months, few visitors came to see them. "George Prescott," he says, "sometimes enters our paradise to bring us the products of the soil, but for weeks the snow in our avenue has been untrodden by any other guest." Mrs. Hawthorne's letters at this period are exceedingly interesting, for nowhere in her husband's writings, or in those of others, do we come so close to this rare and remarkable man. The following description of his character seems to have been a genuine case of thought transferrence, so much is it like his own writing in grace and purity of expression:

"He loves power as little as any mortal I ever knew; and it is never a question of private will between us, but of absolute right. His conscience is too fine and high to permit him to be arbitrary. His will is strong, but not to govern others. He is so simple, so transparent, so just, so tender, so magnanimous, that my highest instinct could only correspond to his will. I never knew such delicacy of nature."

This is a classic gem, and nothing could be added to it. The character of Hilda in "The Marble Faun," is simply Mrs. Hawthorne at the age of twenty-two. She was a pure-hearted, unselfish person, but not self-reliant or over wise. There is a golden edge or rainbow hue to his description of the old manse which distinguishes it from his other writings and betrays the deeply penetrating happiness he felt there. It is like a morning landscape painted while the dew is on the grass. One notices especially his delight in the great yellow squash-blossoms and the way in which he idealizes them. This, and the three years he spent in Europe after the expiration of his consulate, were the holidays of his life and the reward of all the rest.

With the exception of William Ellery Channing, he made no friends in Concord, though he speaks kindly of Thoreau, and compares Channing to him. It is to be suspected that this was largely on account of his political principles—or the lack of them. He had held office under a democratic administration and felt that his interests were connected with that party. Further than that, he does not appear to have distinguished between the two parties. Of his most intimate friends, one was a democrat and the other a whig. But the annexation of Texas was now in sight, and Concord was stirred again with the spirit of '75. Hawthorne, as is well known, did not take interest in the antislavery movement, and a heated discussion of any subject must have been jarring and unpleasant to him.

It is not impossible that in this way he came into conflict with Margaret Fuller and conceived an abiding dislike to her. Miss Fuller would not have spared her eloquence in regard to what she considered a matter of principle, nor is it likely that she would have been more considerate of the respect which is due in such matters from a woman to a man.

There were not a few persons whom she offended by too much "bounce." To a reverend gentleman who asked her, as they were parting at the house of a mutual friend, where her office was in Boston, she replied, "Oh! look in the directory for it"; instead of politely giving him the street and number. Thus she lost a pleasant acquaintance and a subscriber to "The Dial." Hawthorne and his wife had not been four days in Concord before she came to them with a proposition that they should take Ellery Channing and his wife, who was her own sister, into their family as boarders. One cannot help some astonishment at this proceeding, for it is an instinct with all women to know that a newly married couple do not like to be interfered with. No word has ever been published from which we can infer how the grievance between them originated, but it is morally certain that there was a grievance of some kind, and as Hawthorne was the most inoffensive of men, it is not likely that he was responsible for it.

Now in regard to what follows, it is well to carry in mind two important points. In the first place, a writer of fiction acquires a habit, very naturally, of dealing with all tales and anecdotes as if they were subjects for his art, and is not therefore so accurate a judge of their veracity as a lawyer or a critic might be. Whatever holds together as a story is to him as good as true. The second point is that although Hawthorne understood human nature better than the rest of us, it is nevertheless with certain limitations. His romance characters are of a rare sort and are well sustained, but they form a group by themselves. He has not the range of Scott, Thackeray, or Goethe. There is not the slightest evidence that he appreciated the character of Emerson; and if so, he would not be likely to appreciate Emerson's intimate friends. A man like John Brown, always ready to rush upon destruction for an idea, must have been an inexplicable riddle to him. Yet John Brown was the only American who could match Hawthorne in ideality — totally different as they were in other respects.

Twelve years later, while Hawthorne was in Rome, he became acquainted with a sculptor named Mosier, who gave him a most disparaging account of Margaret Fuller's marriage to Count D'Ossoli. This informant said that the D'Ossoli family, though pretending to be noble, actually lived like peasants; that the count's brother had for some years been a servant to a gentleman he knew of; that the count himself was an exceedingly handsome man, but ignorant and clownish; that he could not even speak Italian; and that Margaret Fuller had become a good deal demoralized in Rome, and could neither write nor converse with her former brilliancy. Hawthorne accepted this statement and entered it in his diary with inferences of his own which are still more unfavorable to Miss Fuller.

We like to believe that he wrote this rather to relieve his own mind than with the expectation of influencing the minds of others. We can easily forgive him for it, for in the whole course of his life there is no other instance of the same kind; but he was most certainly in error to believe such an imputation on the character of a respectable lady from the authority of a single witness. C. P. Cranch, the poet and landscape-painter, says that this Mr. Mosier was the veriest Munchausen, and nobody in Rome thought of crediting his stories. But Mosier's statement shows on its face signs of internal weakness. When he says that Count D'Ossoli in attempting to model a foot placed the big-toe on the wrong side, he states what is altogether incredible, and discloses his own splenetic humor. Neither is it more likely that Margaret Fuller permitted him to examine her manuscripts so that she might obtain his assistance in regard to their publication. Whatever may be said of her, she was not a fool, and was better acquainted with both English and American publishers than all the sculptors in Italy.

Miss Fuller's marriage was rather a peculiar one, but nothing is more common than for a highly intellectual woman to select a mate who is a decided contrast to her. Hawthorne has given us an example of this in the romance of Monte Beni—the brilliant Miriam falling in love with that Italian child of nature Donatello. Margaret Fuller was always attracted strongly by personal beauty, and when she was a girl at school she chose her favorites rather for that than for their mental endowments. The handsome D'Ossoli was no doubt all the more interesting to her because he belonged to a noble family which had come to misfortune. Is it not better for us to look at the matter in this way? Margaret Fuller's marriage, voyage, and final destruction against the rocks of her native land, would form the subject for a magnificent poem.

How could it happen that Hawthorne deceived himself? Is it possible that he was in the right, and men like Emerson, Ripley, and James Freeman Clarke in the wrong? Why does he consider Miss Fuller to have had a strong, coarse nature, and to have been morally unsound? Here we enter into the deepest recesses of the author's nature.

Hawthorne was not wholly a fatalist, or he never could have conceived the character of Donatello, but he was very largely so. A man for whom a life of action is impossible, and who is thus unable to escape wholly from his own shadow, naturally comes to look on any series of events as an inevitable chain of cause and effect. He speaks somewhere of Byron's virtues and vices as being so closely interwoven that he could not have had one without the other, and if the objectionable passages in his poetry were expurgated, the life and genius of it would go with them. His story of "The Birth-mark" is an allegory of the same description. He did not agree with Shakspeare, that the best men are moulded out of faults, but believed that as we are in the beginning, so we remain essentially till the end.

He says that whenever Margaret Fuller heard of a rare virtue, she wished to possess it and adorn herself with it; so that she finally became a sort of brilliant external patchwork, dazzling to the eye, but internally quite different. There is a certain truth in this, but it is not a whole truth; for there is Socrates—a compendium of all the ancient virtues, consistent throughout, and who formed himself in the manner Hawthorne describes. It is true that in a search after rare and exceptional virtues we are apt to lose sight of the more homely kind which form the bone and sinew of human-life. But is not this effort a virtue in itself? Is not all progress in this world accomplished as the frog escaped from the well, by jumping up three feet and falling back two? Is not the very crown of character that which we derive from failure, penitence, and self-reproach? Human nature is a mysterious labyrinth and the wisest have only found a partial clue to it.

George S. Hillard—a brilliant amateur sort of writer, orator and editor—came to visit Hawthorne one of the last Sundays while he remained in the Old Manse, and the two went together to spend the forenoon in Walden woods, calling on Emerson by the way to inquire what the best road might be. Emerson prudently detained them until after the townspeople were safely in their churches, and then accompanied them. It is a pleasant retrospect to think of those two mighty men, so like and yet so unlike, together with their amiable and gifted friend, going off on this Sunday excursion. Mr. Hillard was a fortunate companion for him, for no one could serve better as a mean between two extremes. At the close of Hawthorne's rehearsal of this episode, he makes this note, in commentary:—

"I find that my respect for clerical people, as such, and my faith in the utility of their office, decrease daily. We certainly do need a new Revelation, a new system; for there seems to be no life in the old one."

Was this the summary and net result of their stroll in Walden woods? It must be confessed that such was the opinion of the most thoughtful and high-minded people in those days; but we do not feel so now. Schism and separation have done their work, and liberal thinkers everywhere are now returning to the Christian fold.

* * * * *

About the first of June 1860 the Hawthorne family returned from their long residence in England and Italy. There was no little curiosity concerning them in the quiet old settlement, which was increased by the fact that nothing was seen of them for several months after they came.

If Thoreau was a recluse, Hawthorne was an anchorite. He brought up his children in such purity and simplicity as is scarcely credible,—not altogether a wise plan. It was said that he did not even take a daily paper. In the following year Martin F. Conway, the first United States representative from Kansas, went to Concord to call on Emerson, and Emerson invited Hawthorne to dine with them. Judge Conway afterwards remarked that Mr. Hawthorne said very little during the dinner, and whenever he spoke he blushed. Imagine a man five times as sensitive as a young lady in her first season, with the will of a Titan, and a mind like a crown-glass mirror, and you have Nathaniel Hawthorne. While he was in a state of observation, the expression of his face reflected everything that was going on about him; in his reflective moods, it was like looking in at the window of a dark room, or perhaps a picture-gallery; and if any accident disturbed him his look was something like a cracked pane of glass.

Moreover there was something unearthly or superterrestrial about him, as if he had been born and brought up in the planet Saturn. Wherever he went he seemed to carry twilight with him. He walked in perfect silence looking furtively about for fear he might meet some one that he knew. His large frame and strong physique ought to have lasted him till the year 1900. There would seem to be something strange and mysterious about his death, as there was in his life. His head was massive, and his face handsome without being attractive. [Footnote: This, however, was near the close of his life.] The brow was finely chiseled, and the eyes beneath it were dark, luminous and fathomless. I never saw him smile, except slightly with his eyes.

If his son invited a friend to dinner it was always when his father was away from home. Neither do I remember seeing him at his daughter's out-coming party,—an occasion when the town musician declined to appear because the sister of his particular friend had not been invited.

Emerson has given an account of this trait in Hawthorne's character, but he has failed to discover the mainspring of it. Who indeed can explain it? It was part of the man, and without it we could not have had Hawthorne. Perhaps the easiest solution is that of Thoreau's wild apple-tree. When the sprout from an apple-seed comes up in the grass a cow pretty soon bites it off. The next year it puts out two more shoots, and the ends of these are again nipped off. Thus it continues to grow under severe restrictions and forms at length a large thorn-bush, from which finally the tree is able to shoot up beyond the cow's reach and bears its proper fruit. So no doubt

Hawthorne in his youth, being a tender plant, was greatly annoyed by brutal and inconsiderate people. A sensitive, proud and refined nature inevitably becomes a target for all the cheap wits and mischievous idlers in the neighborhood. To escape from this we may suppose that Hawthorne surrounded himself with an invisible network of reserve, behind which his pure and lofty spirit could develop itself in a harmonious manner.

This he certainly succeeded in doing. In purity of expression and a graceful diction Hawthorne takes the lead of his century. He was the romance writer of the Anglo-Saxon race; in that line only Goethe has surpassed him. Nor is it possible for pure and beautiful work to emanate from a mind which is not equally pure and beautiful. Wells of English undefiled cannot flow from a turbid spring.

In purity Emerson probably equaled him, but not in his sense of beauty. Where he surpassed Hawthorne was in manliness, and in his broad humanitarian interests. Otherwise no two men could be more unlike than these, and it would seem to be part of the irony of fate that they should have lived on the same street, and been obliged to meet and speak with each other. One was like sunshine, the other shadow. Emerson was transparent, and wished to be so, he had nothing to conceal from friend or enemy. Hawthorne was simply impenetrable. Emerson was cordial and moderately sympathetic. Hawthorne was reserved, but his sympathies were as profound as the human soul itself. To study human nature as Hawthorne and Shakespeare did, and to make models of their acquaintances for works of fiction, Emerson would have considered a sin; while the evolution of sin and its effect on character was the principal study of Hawthorne's life. One was an optimist, and the other what is sometimes unjustly called a pessimist: that is, one who looks facts in the face and sees people as they are. Hawthorne could not have felt quite comfortable in the presence of a man who asked such searching questions as Emerson frequently did, and Emerson could scarcely have found satisfaction in conversing with one who never had any opinion to express.

A good many people claimed to have been Hawthorne's friends after his death who were sufficiently afraid of him while he was alive. He does not appear to have ever had but two very intimate friends, Franklin Pierce and George S. Hillard, both remarkably amiable and sympathetic men,— qualities to which they owed equally their successes and failures in life. Ex-president Pierce used to come to Concord and carry Hawthorne off to the White Mountains, the Isles of Shoals or Philadelphia, just as two college-students will drop their books and go off somewhere to have a good time. Once while Hawthorne was in Boston, Mr. Hillard tried to persuade him to go to Cambridge and dine with Longfellow; but he would not, and went home by the next train.

He was pro-slavery in politics, partly because his two friends were so, and partly because he disliked the abolitionists. It is not necessary to suppose that the pro-slavery people of the North in those days believed that human slavery was morally right. It is doubtful if any one believed that. A great many considered it, as Webster did, a serious evil but a dangerous matter to interfere with (and so it proved); some were influenced by mercenary motives; and the northern Democrats, misled by the illogical doctrine of State Sovereignty, believed they had no right to interfere with it. Mr. Hillard held the first of these positions, and General Pierce the last. Very likely Hawthorne shared in both of them; but he never explained himself, and what he thought on the subject will always remain a mystery. The political element seems almost to have been left out of his composition; and in one of his books he speaks of the Concord fight with a certain kind of indifference.

Alcott was almost the only man in Concord who had the courage to call on Hawthorne. Sometimes they even went to walk together. How much satisfaction Hawthorne found in these visits it would be difficult to say, for the very philosophic breadth and extension of Alcott's interest were enough to make Hawthorne feel rather shy of him. Alcott's conversation about books and literature was often very fine, but even this could not have given Hawthorne much entertainment. His own library, as he states himself somewhere, was of a miscellaneous character, and contained the works of scarcely any author of repute except Shakespeare. Alcott's sense of humor and keen knowledge of human nature may have been a sort of common ground between them.

Meanwhile Hawthorne, as afterwards appeared, was making a study of Alcott to see whether he would serve his purpose as the mainspring for a new work of fiction. The manuscript plot of a romance was found among Hawthorne's papers in which he describes a personage in general outline like his neighbor Alcott, but without his ideality and good-humor. This imaginary character was supposed to live in a retired manner, together with an old housekeeper, a boy of whom he is the legal guardian, and a huge spider in which his interest and solicitude are more especially centred. What the catastrophe of this strange story was to have been, we are not informed, but it naturally would have arisen from the unhealthy and oppressive social position in which the boy must have found himself as he advanced towards manhood. At the close of his memoranda Hawthorne says, "In person and figure Mr. Alcott—". To be selected as the mainspring of a romance is properly a compliment.

There was a certain Dutch artist who made a specialty of sheep, and painted them so well that Goethe said of him, "This painter so entered into the life of his subject that I think he must have been a sheep, and I shall become one if I continue to look at his pictures." In the same way Hawthorne had such penetrating sympathy for all living things, that he unconsciously absorbed certain qualities from those with which he was most familiar. He would sometimes write a letter to his publisher, Mr. Fields, which was almost like what Mr. Fields would have written to him.

Venomous creatures appeared to have been especially interesting to him, and he even fancied a poisonous influence in the Roman sunshine. Perhaps his liking for spiders may account for a certain cobwebby feeling which comes over one at times while reading his books. There can be no doubt of this, for when I once spoke of it, a lawyer who was present replied, "I have said the same myself; and when I was in Paris reading a French newspaper, I had a feeling as if cobwebs were being drawn across my face, and looking down to the end of the column, I saw that it was a translation from Hawthorne." But these peculiarities are like the soil which gives flavor to the grape, and the wine that comes from the grape.

If the reader thinks that in these few paragraphs Hawthorne has hardly received proper justice, he may not be far wrong. Yet how can any personal account of such a man do him justice. It may be said of him that he was a model husband, a kind father, and an exemplary citizen, and that is all. During his lifetime there were people who did him great injustice. His reserved life was looked upon as a morbid selfishness. The rare publication of his writings was supposed to arise from indolence. It was thought that he wrote the life of Franklin Pierce for the sake of a government office, and when he was actually appointed consul at Liverpool, the case was proved beyond a doubt. The anti-slavery people looked upon him as a lamentable exception to the other literary men of America, who were all on their side: they doubted if he had been born with any sense of right and wrong. What answer can be made to such accusations? When it is a question of motive, of moral consciousness, how are such charges to be refuted?

So President Garfield has often been accused of appointing an efficient and honest collector for the port of New York, in the interest of mercenary politics. Charles Sumner for preventing the annexation of San Domingo, was called a traitor to the negro race, and it was said that his speech on the subject was delivered under the influence of brandy. A college-professor informed his class that Sumner was a man of small erudition, and Garrison spoke of him as one who had evidently joined the anti-slavery cause from interested motives. A Boston merchant whose word had been as good as his note for thirty years was gibbetted soon after his death by a high-minded journalist, as the type of mendacious duplicity.

But why multiply these unpleasant examples of misrepresentation? Hardly a great and good man has ever lived without suffering from it at one time or another. They originate in bad temper, in partisan malice, and those believe them who have no just criterion to distinguish truth from falsehood.

After all, what other American has accomplished a literary work equal to Hawthorne's. He was an artist, purely an artist, and of the finest quality. The raw material may be in us, but to develop it requires pains and labor. The greater the talent the more difficult is its fruition. Hawthorne's life was absorbed in this. His habitual mood was a dreamy, brooding observation. When Englishmen say that no great work of art has been produced in America; that Allston's magnificent pictures remain half-finished; that neither Emerson or Lowell has been able to write a book, but only essays; that we have no historian as good as Macaulay, and that the best of our poetry consists of ballads and other short pieces; my reply is, "The Scarlet Letter" and "The Marble Faun." These are great works of art. The most unique and original, perhaps, of the present century; and if they have not the lyrical form they are exquisitely written, and none the less poetic.

There is a difference in kind between a great work and a small one. A good sonnet may be finished in an hour, and is a pleasant recreation; but the composition of a tragedy requires a severe, protracted and laborious effort. Goethe's finest songs were written in a moment, a flash of inspiration; but Faust may be called the work of his lifetime. He himself describes the difficulties which attend the composition of a tragedy, in such a manner as may well deter others from attempting it. How few, indeed, are the dramatic poets in all times and countries! Even Byron did not succeed in this. Mrs. Hawthorne said that during the period while her husband was occupied with the "Scarlet Letter," there were a contraction of his brow, and a look of care and anxiety in his face, which were reflected in her own nerves and made her unhappy, although she knew little of what he was writing. Both these romances are tragedies; and there is something in tragedy that places it at the top of all literature. Their subjects also indicate that he was in full sympathy with his own time, and perhaps understood the nineteenth century better than it does itself.

Emerson has been called a Greek, but Hawthorne was more Hellenic than he. This may be perceived in his version of the Greek legends in "Tanglewood Tales." His style is much like that of Isocrates. Where Webster or Emerson would use Saxon words, Hawthorne would use Greek or Latin ones, and gain in grace and flexibility what he lost in force and vigor. He would seem to have been a southerner by nature, fond of warm weather and an inactive life.

His short stories are of equal value comparatively with those that are longer and more complete. I remember in my youth being attracted by the title of one of them. It was called "The Unpardonable Sin," and described a man, who, having spent many years in search of this iniquity, finds it too heavy a burden for his soul to carry, and destroys himself one night in a limekiln. Next morning the lime-burner discovered a marble heart floating on the surface of the seething lime. This was the unpardonable sin, — to have a cold, unfeeling heart. Such allegories make a more lasting impression than many sermons. His note-books also are of great value, especially the American ones. He makes dramatic situations out of the simplest incidents, and we read between the lines sentences he never wrote. We remember them without in the least intending to do so, and find ourselves reflecting upon them as if they were important events. No writer since Fielding has given so faithful a picture of the time in which he lived.

One can envy such a man the three years he spent in Italy. During that time he resided chiefly in a villa on the height called Bellosguardo, near Florence, a villa which he has described with some changes, in the "Marble Faun," as the mountain residence of Donatello. A more delightful summer abode cannot be conceived, for it has the advantage of mountain air, and the view from it is unsurpassable. Picturesque Florence, with its towers and battlements, lies almost beneath it, while the green and sylvan valley of the Arno stands before it, with the far-off purple mists of the Mediterranean. Behind it the Apennines stretch from Livorno to Rome. The interior of this chateau, finished in ancient marble, he has described himself.

Hawthorne's life was not a very easy one, as judged by ordinary standards; and until he went to England it was a weary and uncomfortable struggle. Let us be thankful that for once he had a full measure of rest and enjoyment, and let us be grateful to the man who made this possible for him.

More than ten years after his death on a summer afternoon Mr. Alcott was entertaining some friends, and as they looked towards the Hawthorne house one of them said, "Would you be surprised, Mr. Alcott, to see Nathaniel Hawthorne some day gliding past your rustic fence as he used to do?" "No, sir, I should not," replied the old philosopher, "for while he lived he always seemed to me like an apparition from some other world. I used to see him coming down from the woods between five and six o'clock, and if he caught sight of any one in the road he would go under cover like a partridge. Then those strange suspicious side-glances of his! They are not anywhere in his writings. I believe they were inherited from some ancestor who was a smuggler, or perhaps even an old pirate. In his investigation of sin he was expiating the sins of his progenitors." There is reason for believing that Alcott was not far wrong in this conjecture.

Julian Hawthorne, in the biography of his father, says of their ancestors: "His forefathers, whatever their less obvious qualities may have been, were at all events enterprising, active, practical men, stern and courageous, accustomed to deal with and control lawless and rugged characters; they were sea-captains, farmers, soldiers, magistrates; and, in whatever capacity, they were used to see their iron will prevail, and to be answerable to no man."

A man who does not subordinate his will to the common law and the common good must eventually become a lawless man; unless restrained by such natural refinement and rare sense of propriety as we meet with in Hawthorne himself. It is not necessary to suppose that any of them were pirates, which was probably a mere flourish of Alcott's rhetoric.

* * * * *

There is another legend that Daniel Webster, Rufus Choate and Nathaniel Hawthorne were all distantly related through the Batchelder family. There are said to be red and black Batchelders, like the Douglas family in Scotland; and the black Batchelders have a rare gift of intellect which only comes to the surface when united with some other stock. One would like to know how much truth there is in this. There are indeed certain striking points of resemblance between these three; each in his own line surpassing all others of the same period. Their complexion, and their great physical strength, their deeply arched eye-brows, their genius for language, their reticent and contemplative habits, and especially a certain pregnant gloominess of expression, would seem to indicate a nearer unity than the general one of the Aryan races. Yet the case remains to be proven by documentary evidence.

LOUISA M. ALCOTT

Mr. Alcott's house in Concord was situated on the Lexington road about three-quarters of a mile from the village centre. It was the best-looking house almost in the town, being of simple but faultless architecture, while the others were mostly either too thin or too thick, or out of proportion in some way. It lacked a coat of fresh paint sometimes, but this was to its advantage from an artistic point of view. Fine old elm-trees shaded the path in front of it, and across the road a broad level meadow stretched away to Walden woods. In the rear it was half surrounded by low pine-wooded hills, which protected it from the north-easterly storms and the cold draughts of winter. Mr. Alcott had quite a genius for rustic architecture, as is proved by the summer-house which he and Thoreau built for Emerson, and the fences, seats and arbors with which he adorned his little place added a final charm to the rural picture. In summer nights the droning of the bittern could be heard across the meadows, and woodcock came down familiarly from the hills to look for worms in the vegetable-garden. The snow melted here in Spring and the grass grew green earlier than in other places. It was the fitting abode and haven of rest for a family that had found the conflict of life too hard for them.

Within the house was as pleasant as without. There is no better decoration for a room than a good library, and though Mr. Alcott's books were not handsomely bound one could see at a glance they were not of a common sort. They gave his study an air of distinction, which was well carried out by the refined look and calm demeanor of its occupant. The room opposite, which was both parlor and living-room, always had a cheerful homelike appearance; and after the youngest daughter May entered on her profession as a painter, it soon became an interesting museum of sketches, water-colors and photographs. I remember an engraving of Murillo's Virgin, with the moon under her feet, hanging on the wall, and some excellent copies of Turner's water-color studies. The Alcotts were a hospitable family, not easily disturbed by callers, and ready to share what they had with others. The house had a style of its own.

How Emerson accomplished what he did, with his slight physique and slender strength, will always be one of the marvels of biography. His is the only instance, I believe, on record of a man who was able to support a family by writing and talking on abstract subjects. It is true he inherited a small property, enough to support a single man in a modest way, and without this his career would not have been possible; but the main source of his income was winter lecturing—a practice which evidently killed Theodore Parker, naturally a strong and powerful man. Yet he was not satisfied with this, but wished also to provide for others who had no claims of relationship upon him. His generous efforts in behalf of Carlyle have long since been made public; but the help he gave Mr. Alcott will probably never be known. Least of all would Emerson have wished it to be known. One can imagine that he said to himself: "Here is a man of rare spiritual quality, with whom I am in the closest sympathy: I cannot permit him to suffer any longer." So after the philosophic school in the Masonic Temple had come to an end, he invited him to Concord and cared for him like a brother. Mr. Alcott deserved this, for though he was not more a philosopher than Thoreau was a naturalist, and equally with Thoreau he was a character. The primal tenet in his creed was like the ancient mariner's, to harm neither man nor bird nor beast; and he exemplified this doctrine with incredible consistency for full fifty years. He lived a blameless life. Many laughed at him for his unpractical theories; but the example of one such man, even in a reactionary way, is worth more to the community than the practical efforts of ten ordinary men. He has besides the distinction of being the person, whom, during the middle portion of his life, Emerson most liked to converse with.

Froude the historian calls Charles the Fifth one of nature's gentlemen: so was Mr. Alcott. It is easy to distinguish the man whose behavior is an emanation of himself from people of well-bred manners or of cultivated manners. Well-bred manners come from habit and association, and though always pleasant may be nothing more than a superficial varnish; while cultivated manners imply a certain amount of self-restraint. No man was ever more free from formality or affectation. He was neither condescending to inferiors nor would he yield ground to those who considered themselves above him, but met all people on the broad equality of self-respect. He was always most respected where society was most polite and refined. Neither was he lacking in personal courage. During the Anthony Burns excitement in Boston in 1852, he took a prominent position among the rescuers, and if a collision of the guards had taken place he would likely have been killed.

He had a fine philosophical mind, and if it had only been trained properly in early life he might have won a distinguished place among metaphysicians. That however was hardly possible in the America of that time. He was not a philosopher in the modern sense, but he was in the ancient sense—a disciple of Pythagoras, dropped down from the pure Grecian sky into the restless turmoil of the nineteenth century. He wished to discover everything anew for himself, instead of building upon the discoveries of others. His conversations, usually in the parlors of some philanthropic gentlemen, were made up partly of Pythagorean speculation and partly of fine ethical rhapsody which sometimes rose to genuine eloquence. They served to interest neophytes in the operations of their own minds, and the more experienced found much the same satisfaction in it as in Emerson's discourses. He was an excellent speaker; confident, quick-witted and conciliatory. I remember a very eloquent address that he delivered at an anniversary meeting in 1868, and at an anti-slavery convention, where Garrison and Phillips fell out, Mr. Alcott made the best speech of the occasion, discriminating between the two leaders in a just and sensible manner.

He was memorable for shrewd observations. He said once to a lady who was fretting because the clergyman did not cone in time, "Meanwhile, Mrs. D., there is providence." Of a good-humored young radical who wished to make war on all conventional forms, religious and political parties, he remarked, "Unless our friend changes his ideas he will not be the happy man at forty that he is now;" and the saying came true. If we are to judge the value of Alcott's thought by the constant cheerfulness and contentment of his daily life, his ideas must have been of an excellent quality. His flowing white hair, and the calmness and purity of his aspect, gave him quite an apostolic look; and once while visiting at the house of a friend, a certain small boy—the same for whom John Brown afterwards wrote his autobiography of a boy—asked his mother if that man was one of Christ's disciples. Such was the father of "Little Women."

The Alcotts received their friends weather permitting on Monday evenings, and some favored youths of Mr. Sanborn's school would go there to play whist, make poker-sketches, and talk with the ladies; while Mrs. Alcott, who had played with the famous automaton in her younger days, would have a quiet game of chess with some older person in a corner. Louisa usually sat by the fire-place, knitting rapidly with an open book in her lap, and if required to make up a table would come forward with a quiet look of resignation and some such remark as "You know I am not a Sarah Battles." Then after a while her love of fun would break forth, and her bright flashes of wit would play about the heads of all who were in the room. Just after ten Mr. Alcott would come in with a dish of handsome apples and his wife produce some ginger cakes; a lively chat for fifteen or twenty minutes would follow, and then the guests would walk home. It was in this way Louisa acquired that stock of information about young people and their affairs which she made such good use of afterwards. Human nature to the poet and novelist is like a Calumet and Hecla mine which never becomes exhausted.

Louisa Alcott resembled her mother in figure, features and color, and in her ardent and impulsive temperament. In the greater number of families the eldest child resembles the father; the second and third are more like their mother, and the fifth (if there be so many) is often like the grandparents. In the Alcott family however it was just the reverse of this, for May the youngest daughter was the only one like her father, inheriting the artistic side of his nature, instead of the philosophical. Neither did Louisa resemble her grandmother's family, the Sewalls. She was emphatically a May, and the best of all the Mays, though there have been many of them who were excellent. I think she was indebted to her father for her enterprising spirit and keen sense of character. Mr. Alcott knew the people of Concord much better than they understood him, and was always most interesting when he talked of the distinguished people with whom he had been acquainted. May was fond of society, and a walk to and from the school dances cold winter nights; and then ready next morning for a skating party on Walden pond; but she said her sisters had little entertainment in their youth, dressing always in the plainest manner and practising a stoical self-denial. Louisa liked to look at other people dancing, and generally it made her happy to see the young folks enjoy themselves. This shows the true woman in her. The portrait she has given of herself as Jo in "Little Women" is not to be taken too literally. Like Thackeray in "Pendennis" she has purposely left out the noble side of her nature,—for indeed that was only disclosed at rare intervals and for those who had eyes to see. She had the strongest features of the family, and a quick decisive manner which was sometimes mistaken for arrogance.

Louisa and her sister Annie (now Mrs. Pratt) were excellent actresses, and were always in demand when private theatricals were on foot. To see them perform in the "Two Buzzards" with her sister and F. B. Sanborn was a treat of the first order. I can hear Louisa now saying, "Brother Benjamin, brother Benjamin!" in a scene of which all the rest is gone from my memory. Another favorite *role* of hers was Dickens' character of Sarah Gamp in the nocturnal interview with her friend Betsy Prig. As Mrs. Jarley exhibiting her wax tableaux she was inimitable. She did it with a snap. Once she was called upon to assist at an entertainment given at the house of the village blacksmith: she invented a charade which was both novel and appropriate. She arranged her father to look like the Boston statue of Franklin—and the resemblance was a very striking one—and then came in with another gentleman in a travelling dress, and surveyed and criticized him. When she said, "He seems to have rather a brassy expression," Mr. Alcott could scarcely hold his face. This was the first part: the second consisted of the scene from the "Two Buzzards" already mentioned, and for the third a witty dialogue about Mr. Sanborn's school. As more than half of the audience was composed of Mr. Sanborn's pupils this charade produced a great effect.

Her acting had this peculiarity, that she seemed always to be herself and the character she was representing at the same time. This is the case also with some professional actors and actresses, notably with Madame Ristori and Edwin Booth: but it is not the finest kind of acting.

The anti-slavery conflict and the civil-war with which it ended appealed strongly to her ardent and sympathetic nature; and this finally resulted in her enlisting as a nurse to tend the wounded soldiers. Her lively and picturesque "Hospital Sketches" written at Washington for the "Boston Commonwealth" are the echo of this period. Very few passed through that crisis without bearing the scars of it for life, and the fever which Louisa Alcott contracted in the camp sapped her vitality and probably shortened her days. She was one of the veterans, and deserved a pension.

While she was convalescing she said to a friend who condoled with her on her misfortunes, "The loss of my hair was the worst of it" (this had been cut off by order of the doctor); "I felt as if that were a disgrace." When some one asked her how she amused herself she replied, "I think out sketches of stories and put them away in little pigeon-holes in my brain for future use."

On the Fourth of July 1864 there was an evening-party at the house of Hon. E. R. Hoar, and nearly at the close of it Miss Alcott came to me with a humorous twinkle in her eye and said: "A few of us are going to have a picnic to-morrow at Conantum"—a picturesque bluff owned by one Conant, about three miles up the river—"and Mrs. Austin and I have engaged a boat for the occasion and are now looking for a muscular heathen to row it. Will you come?" Nothing could have pleased me better; so next morning we all started in the best of spirits. There was however a head wind, the boat was without a rudder, and the Concord River is very crooked. I think Miss May Alcott was also in the party. I found it terribly hard rowing, and finally exclaimed, "This is the darnedest boat I ever pulled." "Frank," said Louisa, "never say darn. Much better to be profane than vulgar. I had rather live in hell than in some places on earth. Strong language, but true. Here, take some cold tea." She had a claret-bottle full of this beverage, and gave me a good drink of it. Her vigorous piece of common-sense was also very refreshing, and Conantum being now in sight, Miss Alcott and her sister insisted on landing at the next bridge, leaving Mrs. Austin [Footnote: Mrs. Jane G. Austin, a bright little story-writer of those days and very much like her English namesake.] and myself to continue the way alone. Unluckily there was no one now to care for the bottle of cold tea, and rolling about in the stern of the boat the cork came out and the tea was spilled. This was a severe loss to Miss Alcott who was not yet strong enough for an all-day picnic, and when I explained it to her she said, "Don't talk to me. I know you college-boys. That cork never came out by accident. You drank the tea yourself, and now in what way I am going to punish you for it I cannot tell." With such biting humor she partly relieved and partly concealed her just vexation.

Characteristic writers are commonly the last to be appreciated, and Miss Alcott's first novel did not meet with an encouraging reception from the public. Some tender critics even complained that the story was subversive of conservative morality. "I cannot help that," Louisa remarked in her emphatic manner, "I did not make morality or human nature, and am not responsible for either: but people who are given to moods act as I have described; sometimes they like one person and sometimes another." Perhaps she was thinking not so much of moody natures as of those contradictory characters who have inherited the traits of very dissimilar ancestors. She wrote another novel which she herself liked much better and had great hopes of, which was lost in some miraculous way by her publisher Mr. Fields. He paid her for it what many people would consider a handsome compensation—exactly the sum that Stuart Mill paid Carlyle for burning up the first volume of his "French Revolution"—but it was a trying affair for both sides. How so bulky an object as a novel in manuscript could have been lost without its falling into the hands of some person who knew what to do with it, is most difficult to imagine.

That so many of the world's benefactors are doomed to incalculable torments here on earth may be a good argument for immortality, but for Divine Providence it is no better evidence than the Lisbon earthquake which so startled the optimists and thinking men of the last century. There is no telling why this is so; for misfortune falls upon the just as well as the unjust, and often no human foresight can prevent it. Louisa Alcott supposed that she was nearly well of her fever when inflammatory rheumatism set in. The worst of this was the loss of sleep which it occasioned. Long continued wakefulness is a kind of nervous cremation, and resembles in its physical effect the perpetual drop of water on the head with which the Spanish inquisitors used to torment their heretics. Any mental agitation makes the case very much worse, and it requires great self-control to prevent this. It was melancholy to behold her at that time. Her pallid face, the dark rings about her eyes, and her dreary, hopeless expression might have penetrated the most obdurate heart. "I don't suppose it is going to kill me," she said, "but I shall never get over it. I go to bed at nine o'clock and think steadily of the wood-box in order to keep my mind from more serious subjects."

It is not always darkest before dawn, especially when the moon is on its last quarter, but happily it was so in this instance. Three years later she was in much better health, and had published "Little Women." First the young people read it; then their fathers and mothers; and then the grandparents read it. Grave merchants and lawyers meeting on their way down town in the morning said to each other, "Have you read 'Little Women'"; and laughed as they said it. The clerks in my office read it, so also did the civil engineer, and the boy in the elevator. It was the rage in '69 as "Pinafore" was in '78. It was re-published in London,—a rare compliment for a book of its kind.

Rumors of this unusual success had reached the little household in Concord and filled their home with pleasant expectations; but they had no idea of the extent of it. The evening papers announced on the night before Christmas that Miss Alcott's publishers had sent her that day a very large cheque. There were many glad hearts at this news beside those in the Alcott family; where, I fancy, tears and prayers were not wanting to complete the sacrament. The long struggle was ended, and peace and rest had come at last. Louisa had won a glorious victory, and the laurel wreath was on her brow.

The style of "Little Women" is not classic; but as Goldsmith says in his preface to the "Vicar of Wakefield," "It matters not." It filled a vacant place in American and perhaps also in English literature, and must continue to fill it. Novelists usually take up their characters at the age of twenty-one, or somewhere in the twenties, and there have also been many excellent books written for children; but to describe the transition period between fifteen and twenty there had not as yet been anything adequate—if we partially except Thomas Hughes' sketches of life at Rugby and Oxford. It is a period of life which deserves much more consideration than it often receives. It is the integrating period, during which we make our characters and form those habits of thought and action which mainly determine our destiny. The bloom of youth may conceal this internal conflict, but it is there none the less, and frequently a very severe one. "You have no idea how many trials I have," I once heard a schoolgirl of sixteen say, the perfect picture of health and happiness; and those who remember well their own youth will not be inclined to laugh at this. The tragedy of childhood is the commonest form of tragedy; and youth is a melodrama in which pathos and humor are equally mingled. Those who by some chance have escaped this experience and have had the path of early life made smooth for them, may grow to be thrifty trees but are not likely to bear much fruit. It is for her clear perception of these conditions and her skill and address in dealing with them that Miss Alcott deserves the celebrity that is now attached to her name. Her simple pictures of domestic country life are drawn with a firm and confident hand. They stand out in strong relief, and take their color from her own warmhearted womanly nature. Her characters act unconsciously before us as if we looked at them through a window. In American fiction "Little Women" holds the next place to the "Scarlet Letter" and "Marble Faun."

There is one of Boccaccio's stories which differs so much from the others in closeness of statement and fulness of detail that it is judged to have been an experience of his own. As the critics say, he knew too much about his subject. Louisa Alcott wisely avoided this error. Her characters are always real, but,—in her best work at least,—not realistic. There are people in natural life, full of peculiarities, whom it would take pages to describe, while others can be hit off in a few sentences. Miss Alcott knew that characters of a few simple traits were best suited to her purpose; and she was too good an artist to imitate her model. Her impersonation of herself as Jo was pretty near the truth, but Beth, Amy, and Meg only resemble her sisters in a very general way. If the book were more of a biography it would not be good fiction. Some of the incidents in it were taken from her own or the family experiences, but more are either imaginary or conventional. It is said that her primary intention was to leave Jo in a state of single blessedness, and that Roberts Brothers fairly declined to publish the second volume unless she was married off to somebody. Thus originated the episode of the German Professor, one of the best in the story. Laurie was supposed to have been taken from Julian Hawthorne, because he lived in the next house and was rather an attractive kind of boy. Louisa herself said there was no ground for this: and yet Laurie seems to me a good deal like him.

I remember meeting her at the radical club in Boston in January 1868, and her drawing me into a corner where she told me that she was writing a book for young people and would like to know about the game of cricket. This fixes the time pretty closely when "Little Women" was begun. She was frequently to be seen at the meetings of the radical club, afterwards called the Chestnut Street club, where her father was one of the leading members. She did not care for lectures, but greatly enjoyed listening to the discussion of learned and thoughtful men. It was an era of large designs and great mental activity; and in such periods the best literary work is always accomplished. Once she said (in her father's presence), "It requires three women to take care of a philosopher, and when the philosopher is old the three women are pretty well used up." But at another time she said, "To think of the money I make by writing this trash, while my father's, words of immortal wisdom only bring him a little celebrity." She honored her father, and lived more for him than for anybody else, including herself.

Her journey through Europe was like a triumphal procession. Doors were opened to her everywhere; not the palace of the Rothschilds or the apartments of the ex-Queen of Naples, but those of distinguished artists and literary people. Mr. Healy, the best American painter in Rome, requested permission to paint her portrait. This she consented to, and was rather surprised when he afterwards presented it to her. "I wondered," she said while we were looking at the picture, "what was going to come next; when one day Mr. Healy's daughter appeared with a novel in manuscript which she wished I would give an opinion of. I found it to be good and sent it to my London publisher, who happily published it for her." Posterity ought to be grateful for Healy's little manoeuvre.

The same attentions followed her on her return to Boston; but she did not care for them. She had learned that the satisfaction of good work is the only one which we never have to regret. She was busy with plans for the future, considering especially how she might order and arrange her affairs for the benefit of her family. Ladies whose names she had never heard, came in fine carriages and sent in their cards to her. This amused her very much. "I don't care who their grandfathers and grandmothers were," she said. "John Hancock was my great-great-grandfather, but nobody ever came to see me on his account." If she had leisure she received them: otherwise not. In her next novel, the "Old Fashioned Girl," she introduces herself with the name of Katie King, and says to her young friends: "Beware of popularity; it is a delusion and a snare; it puffeth up the heart of man, and just as one gets to liking the taste of this intoxicating draught, it suddenly faileth."

When "Little Men" was published a rather censorious critic complained that Miss Alcott's boys and girls had no very good manners, and made some inquiry after the insipid "Rollo" books which were in circulation forty years ago. It is true their manners are not of the best, but they are the Concord manners of that period. Were they otherwise they would not be true to life. Very few boys and girls of sixteen have fine manners; and even after they have acquired the art of good behavior in company they continue to act in quite a different fashion towards each other. What else can we expect of them? Exactly the same objection has been made to "School Days at Rugby"; and when some one complained of Goethe that the characters in "Wilhelm Meister" did not belong to good society he replied in verse, "I have often been in society called 'good,' from which I could not obtain an idea for the smallest poem."

Concord was large enough for Thoreau, but not for Louisa Alcott. She had no proclivity for paddling up and down Concord River in search of ideas. She had a broad cosmopolitan mind, and the slow routine of a country-town was irksome to her. She did not care for nature; and the great world was not too large a field of observation for her. Even in Rome she preferred the living image of a healthy bambino to the statue of the gladiator who has been dying in marble for so many centuries. She loved the society of people who were abreast of the times, who could give her fresh thought and valuable information. The books she read were of the most vigorous description. When some one asked her if she had read Mallock's "New Republic" she replied, "I do not read cotemporary writers; only Emerson and the classics." "Louisa," said I, "you speak to my soul." "Do I?" said she, with a tenderness of feeling such as I had never noticed before. Her attachments were strong; but her resentments were of long duration.

EMERSON HIMSELF

Emerson might be seen on his way to the post-office at precisely half-past five every afternoon, after the crowd there had dispersed. His step was deliberate and dignified, and though his tall lean figure was not a symmetrical one, nor were his movements graceful, yet there was something very pleasant in the aspect of him even at a distance. The same has also been said of good statuary, even before we know what is its subject. He knew all the people old and young in the village, and had a kindly word or a smile for every one of them. His smile was better than anything he said. There is no word in the language that describes it. It was neither sweet nor saintly, but more like what a German poet called the mild radiance of a hidden sun. No picture, photograph or bust of Emerson has ever done him justice for this reason; only such a master as Giorgione could have painted his portrait.

Every morning after reading the "Boston Advertiser" he would go to his study, to take up the work of the day previous and cross out every word in it that could possibly be spared. This procedure and his taste for unusual words is what gives the peculiar style to his writing. It was characteristic of him physically and mentally. He had a spare figure; was sparing of speech, sparing of praise, and sparing of time; in all things temperate and stoical. He had an aquiline face, made up of powerful features without an inch of spare territory.

"With beams December planets dart
His keen eye truth and conduct scanned."

His eyes were sometimes exceedingly brilliant; his nose was strong and aquiline; and the lower part of his face, especially the mouth, was notably like the busts of Julius Caesar. His voice was a baritone of rapid inflections, and when he was very much in earnest it changed to a deep bass. He once said, "Whenever I look in the glass I feel a depression of spirits"; but his friends did not feel so. He was always an agreeable object to them, even in his last years when he looked in his study like an old eagle in his eyrie. Mental power is more attractive than beauty even to ladies.

He was a modern Stoic, and carried that kind of life to a high degree of perfection. He sometimes smoked a cigar, and sometimes drank a glass of wine, but the only real luxury he indulged in was dining with the Atlantic

Club once a month in Boston. During his lecturing tours he was the recipient of a great deal of hospitality, and became the objective centre of many a social gathering; but how much he enjoyed this it would be difficult to tell. He was too modest and genuine to like being lionized. He had neither pride, vanity, nor self-conceit; and his great celebrity never weighed heavily upon him, or discovered itself in his manners. In this respect he carried his stoicism a little too far, for he never would permit any one to talk with him about himself, and enthusiastic admirers of his genius commonly met with a rather cold reception. He repelled everything in the shape of a compliment. Dr. Edward Emerson says somewhere that his father was used to eat whatever was set before him with Spartan-like indifference. This mistake may have arisen from the good quality of Mrs. Emerson's housekeeping, and the excellent fare which she provided for her husband and his friends. Emerson wished to bear the hardships of life without complaining, but he also knew that to make life unnecessarily hard is not only unwise but has an injurious effect on character. As he would have said, it is not according to nature. A horse seeks the best of the road, and a cow the freshest grass in the pasture. Studious people and others who live mostly indoors are obliged to be careful of what they eat. You could not call Emerson an epicure, but he knew how to appreciate a fine dinner. Several witnesses have given their testimony in regard to his partiality for what he called "pie." He was also fond of pears; knew the best varieties and the order in which they ripened. He used to say that there is only ten minutes in which a pear is fairly ripe: before that it is too hard and afterwards too soft. His friend Dr. F. H. Hedge once made a similar remark concerning ripe scholars.

Perhaps the most remarkable trait in his character was his absolute self-poise. He had a balanced mind if there ever was one. Carlyle considered the "Conduct of Life" to be Emerson's best book, and there was reason why it should be. It was the subject of all others which he knew most about. Conduct had been the study of his life. Behavior was a fine art with him, cultivated partly from motives of prudence but more for its own sake. From early morning till bed-time he was always the same, always self-possessed. There was no relaxation of it; he was like an athlete in full training. It was difficult to place him in a position where he did not appear to advantage. But he expected nearly as much from others, and had small patience with those who from ignorance or carelessness infringed the rules of etiquette. One of his expressions was, that death or mutilation was the only excuse for being late to dinner. The notion that poets are an unpractical class of people is pure illusion. The lives of our chief American poets will be sufficient to contradict it; if Dante had not been a just governor of Florence and Aeschylus had not fought like a tiger in the battle of Salamis. Bryant was the able editor of a newspaper; Lowell made an excellent ambassador; and Longfellow also had the reputation with his publishers of being a very shrewd man of business. So was Emerson in all things eminently practical. He would sometimes say, "I allow myself to be cheated by one Irishman"; but I do not think he was cheated very much.

In fair weather he always left his books half an hour or so before dinner and walked out, to get fresh-air and see what was going forward on his little place. The poem called "Hamatreya" and many of his best thoughts were evidently suggested by these short excursions. He says in the "Conduct of Life": "The scholar goes into his garden to obtain a juster statement of his thought. He puts down his hand to pull up a weed. Behind that is a second; behind the second is a third; behind the third a fourth; and beyond that a thousand and four." Who can doubt that this was a personal experience with him, as it has been with some others?

There are many anecdotes of his good sense and sagacity, and the following is perhaps equal to any of them. One summer there was a camp-meeting of spiritualists at Walden Pond, and every evening they held an entertainment of speeches, singing and music, to which a small admittance-fee was charged. It happened, however, that the picnic pavilion was situated close to Mr. Emerson's land, and numbers of Concord people went out of curiosity and leaning against his fence heard and saw everything that went on. A committee of spiritualists consequently called on Mr. Emerson and requested permission to collect fees from those who stole their entertainment in this manner. At first thought this might not seem to be unreasonable; but Emerson replied, "No, I have always enjoyed the privilege of walking upon my neighbors' fields, and I cannot now refuse the same right to them." Could a chief justice have decided the case better?

Emerson's *no* was always decisive, and if one person could not induce him to change his mind I do not believe twenty millions would have succeeded in doing so. When he was involved in a lawsuit regarding some property, and the suggestion was made that he should compromise it, he said: "By no means. If it is mine I want the whole of it; if it is not mine I do not want any of it."

He avoided controversies and often showed great tact in escaping from an argument. What he had once published was of no consequence to him, and he cared little whether others liked it or not. If people advanced opinions or judgments with which he disagreed he made a plain statement of the fact and then changed the subject of conversation. Opponents who wished to corner him, and had perhaps set snares for him to fall into, found themselves outwitted by his unfailing desire for peace and harmony.

He went to the polls and voted; he attended town-meetings and political caucuses, but never took an active share in them. The prohibition of liquor, the tariff question, the woman suffrage movement, and other like vexatious matters he left severely alone. I doubt if any one discovered from first to last what his real opinions were on these subjects. At the Boston Radical Club in 1868 he was asked to give an opinion on woman suffrage, and he replied that he had no doubt that when all women had agreed as to what they wanted, what was in fact best for them, they could easily obtain it through the home influence. These he would say are questions of judgment. The slavery question was a matter of principle; and on that point he gave forth no uncertain sound. He did not, however, engage actively in the controversy till the passage of the fugitive-slave bill warned him how seriously the republic was in danger. Then he threw himself into the struggle with all the energy of his nature, and stumped the Middlesex district for the free-soil candidate Dr. Palfrey. In one of his speeches at this time referring to Webster's support of the bill, he forged this terrible figure, "Every drop of blood in the man's veins has eyes that look downward."

The final test of a deep mind is to respect forms and at the same time recognize how little comparatively they are worth. The technical skill of the pianist requires years of laborious effort, and yet it has no value unless he can also appreciate the intention and spirit of the composer whose music he plays. So it is in art, politics, religion,—and all human affairs. When the national government was captured by the slavocracy, and converted in all its branches into an engine for the oppression of the negro race and white laborers as well, Emerson saw clearly that the season of respect for law had passed by, and he celebrated John Brown as the apostle and martyr of a holy cause. This accurate historical penetration on the part of one who knew but little of history is the finest flower in the poet's crown. What he said of John Brown may now seem somewhat exaggerated; but the importance of the event has never been exaggerated.

An argument, however, is not always to be avoided even at such times as we are least inclined for it. In February 1865 the good people of Concord called a town-meeting to consider the advisability of building a new high-school house. Alcott, who held some office connected with the town schools, was strongly in favor of the project, and on his way to the meeting called on Emerson to secure his vote for it. He soon found, however, that he had waked up the wrong person. Emerson, who was finishing his dinner, considered that in time of war retrenchment and economy were first to be thought of, and that the new school-house had better be deferred for three years at least. But Alcott had also good reasons for his opinion, and with all his deference for Emerson in philosophy and literature he did not seem inclined to yield on the present occasion. So the two friends argued the case together with equal good humor and determination, and the discussion had not ceased when they left the house.

The popular legend that during the Mexican war Mr. Alcott refused to pay taxes that supported an unjust invasion, and was imprisoned for this, is so far true; but it can not be true that when Emerson came to visit him in jail to pay the tax-bill he said, "Bronson, why are you here?" and that Alcott answered, "Waldo, why are you not here?"; for they never called each other anything but Mr. Emerson and Mr. Alcott. The story of Emerson's going with Margaret Fuller to see Fanny Ellsler, the danseuse, was a pure invention of the enemy and had not even the corner-stone of a foundation in fact.

Goethe says in his analysis of manners that the man of noble manners may sometimes give way to his emotions, the man of well-bred manners never. Emerson's manners were half way between these two; a fortunate union of natural courtesy and dignified reserve. It was not possible to be familiar with him. They were better than fine manners, or even well-bred manners, for they were so natural and simple as scarcely to attract attention. Yet he was not a man of noble manners, for he never fully acted out himself. Carlyle had noble manners, but was lacking in courtesy.

Emerson's house stands about twenty-five yards from the street, and there is a smooth white-marble walk from his gate to the front-door. This, together with the pine trees he planted for protection against the north wind, had a cool refreshing effect in midsummer, but at other seasons gave the visitor rather a chilly reception. There was something in Emerson himself that reminded one of this white-marble walk; not that he was cold-hearted, far from it, nor was he lacking in tenderness; but warmth of color he had not. He was too purely moral to be altogether human. He never could have written a tragedy, or made a speech like that of John Adams on the question of separation. How could it be otherwise? Can the descendant of five generations of New England clergymen have the same blood in his veins that warmed the hearts of Marshal Ney and Mirabeau? Perpetual constraint and self-denial may strengthen character, but will human nature be better for it in the end?

Constant trimming must finally weaken the tree; and if we consider history we find that the greatest services to mankind have been those ardent, self-forgetful natures who lived in a large, grand manner, and who cared more for the affairs they have in hand than for their reputations or the salvation of their souls. It was not the just and virtuous Aristides but the bold reckless Themistocles who saved Greece from the Persian invasion.

Luther and Shakespeare are brilliant examples of it. Our American poets have all except Poe a high reputation for virtue and good behavior, but I do not find in them the summer climate of Burns or the magnetism of Byron and Heine. There is such a thing as valuing our faults too highly.

Emerson did not like such men, and was apt to do them injustice. He admired Napoleon and Goethe—a generous nature cannot help that—and his estimate of Napoleon's character is the best that has yet been made; but he preferred Lafayette to Mirabeau, considered Caesar wholly lacking in principle, and thought Machiavelli was the fiend incarnate. His friends were like himself, cool-headed and scrupulous; but they were not the persons who cared most for him and appreciated him the best. Such men as Theodore Parker, M. D. Conway, David A. Wasson and Wendell Phillips did more for Emerson almost than his own writings, in spreading his reputation and celebrating his genius. Wherever Phillips and Parker lectured in the west and were asked, as often happened, who were the best of the New England lecturers, they always placed Emerson at the head of the list. They served as mediators between him and the large class of persons who could not readily understand him.

If he was an exacting moralist, he was never a narrow or pettifogging one. It is true he laid down the rule that a young lady had always the right to break off an engagement, but not so a gentleman, for he has the opportunity, which she has not, of making his own choice,—what no man would have said who was aware of the arts and stratagems which women often practise to obtain the man they desire; but he was not generally a censorious man.

He believed firmly in the old saying of every man to his trade. He never preached sermons on week-days; or discoursed on public and private duties; or lectured about self-sacrifice and the necessity of living for others. He believed that such talk did quite as much harm as good. "Do not try to be good," he would say, "but true to yourself." Wisdom was the best of all virtues because it included all. He thought there were cases in which divorce from incompatibility is justifiable. When a certain transcendentalist left his wife and children in Newport, and came to Concord to write poetry and live the life of an old bachelor, there were many who blamed him severely; but Emerson said, "He is no doubt to blame, but you cannot tell how much; perhaps this is the only way in which he can live." So that there was a large portion of liberality mixed with his natural severity.

Literature is the most satisfactory of all professions, but it is also the most difficult to succeed in. The high-minded writer easily finds themes congenial to his own lofty thoughts, and in the contemplation of these and the companionship of fine books he escapes the weariness and loneliness which often pursue those who are engaged in the busiest avocations. His life is like working in a rose-garden: beautiful images are always before him. His time is his own: he can arrange his own hours for study, rest, and recreation. Especially he can avoid the friction and annoyance of dealing with rude and uncongenial people.

But how is he to persuade others to take an interest in these subjects? The currents of men's thoughts run in certain habitual channels, and to change their course, as every writer who becomes popular is sure to do, is sometimes as great an undertaking as changing the bed of a river. It requires many years for some to be appreciated, and others never are. "We know those who have reached the goal, but who can tell how many have fallen by the way?" Emerson's term of probation, however, was a short one. More fortunate than many, there was a demand for him before he came. Besides the so-called transcendental movement carried him forward in a swift current. He said of it: "At first everybody laughed at me. Then I had ten readers; then a hundred; and then a thousand." And those who laughed at him at first were his most devoted admirers after he had become famous.

If Emerson had not inherited a good property early in life, his career would hardly have been possible. He never was able to publish more than a third of what he wrote, and his books were not a source of large profit to him. He was obliged to make up the deficiency by lecturing. With what fortitude he did this, considering his slender physique, travelling long distances in the coldest weather over such railroads as then were, with a dismal hotel and bad food at the end of every journey, will always be remembered of him. No wonder that he consoled himself with such maxims as, "No man has ever estimated his own troubles too lightly," and such verses as, "Cast the bantling on the rock." Truly it was severe discipline. At Niagara Falls in 1863 the hotel caught fire and Emerson rushed forth at midnight, manuscripts in hand, as Caesar formerly swam with his "Commentaries" from a sinking vessel. The compensation for it was that in this way he made the acquaintance of many interesting and distinguished persons. It also added to his celebrity.

He was the same under all circumstances. It has been said that in his poems we feel the essayist; but perhaps even more we recognize the poet in his essays. So too in his conversation at table and in the parlor, there was something that reminded one of the lecturer: when he appeared on the platform before his audience he was always the plain country gentleman. He affected no graces of oratory, and shunned everything like rhetorical flourish. He was the first of our public speakers to introduce this improvement which has since found its way into the court-room and the theatre. His manner was direct, terse and earnest, with an habitual pause or hesitation to select just the right verb or adjective that would convey the idea he wished to express. His delivery was suited to his thought. His hearers were not commonly pleased with it at first, but if they continued to listen most of them came to have a great liking for it. He had a habit of pausing now and then and turning over the pages before him, as if he had lost his place or was looking for a passage which he could not find; but he never made any explanation for it, and his own family did not know the reason. It may have been done to rest himself; or perhaps to give time for his ideas to settle in the minds of his audience. Some people were foolishly annoyed by it; but not those who understood him. He used to say that either a speaker commands his audience, or his audience commands him.

He was the best lecturer of his time: the one who wore the best. Between 1860 and 1870 he gave four courses of lectures in Boston which were well and profitably attended. No one else could have done this, except perhaps Agassiz. There were others who drew larger houses, but the quality was not so good. Very rarely have such cultivated and intellectual audiences been brought together. A few of his most ardent admirers used to carry opera-glasses with them in order to watch the expression of his face.

William Robinson, the ablest political critic of that time, wrote in 1868, "In spite of an increased hesitation in his delivery Emerson is of all men the one most worth hearing, even better than Phillips and his matchless oratory." He had the most telling way of saying a thing, and knew how to give their full force to his wonderfully brilliant sentences. These would sometimes electrify his hearers, as people are roused on the announcement of some great and fortunate event.

He liked the society of statesmen, scientists, business men, railroad managers, of all who could tell him about what was going on in the world—something, he complained, that the newspapers would not do for him. He preferred their society to that of other poets and scholars. Though an unlimited reader of books he was not properly a scholar himself, and perhaps he felt his own limitation too much in their company.

He studied little at college and it is doubtful if he afterwards made a thorough and systematic investigation of any subject. He was called a philosopher, but he knew little more than the outlines of metaphysics. He could read French fairly, but Latin was the only language with which he was well acquainted. Carlyle tried to persuade him to study German. He did not believe in study, but in the inspiration of nature. This did well enough for him, but he made a mistake in applying the same principle to others.

He was wont to excuse Alcott's rambling rhapsodical conversations on the ground that it was the only talent the man had, that he must do that or nothing; but many people considered that Emerson was more to blame in the matter than Alcott himself. A person who makes a profession of philosophy, as Alcott certainly did, ought to be well acquainted with the writings of other philosophers of his own time; and it surely would have done no harm for Emerson to have suggested this to him. When the Boston Radical Club was formed Emerson thought it would be a good opportunity for Alcott to place his ideas before the public, but Alcott found himself at a disadvantage among the scholarly minds he encountered there.

At the close of his essay on Plato Emerson says, "I am sorry to see him after so many fine thoughts throwing a little mathematical dust in our eyes." Does he partially expose here a peculiarity in his literary procedure? Other people do not read Plato for his fine thoughts, though there are many such, but for the charm of his discourse and his beautiful exposition of Greek Philosophy. From this and from hints let fall in conversation we may suspect that he read books not so much for what was in them as for ideas which they suggested to him, and which he might make use of in his essays and lectures. Alcott said that he carried slips of paper with him on which to jot down these considerations by the way. Thus he came to value books too much from a single point of view, and his friends were sometimes surprised at what he recommended them to read. He would estimate a second-rate novel like "Christie Johnstone" above Thackeray's "Newcomes."

However, it may generally be said that the greater and more high-minded an author might be the better was Emerson a judge of him. He liked in a writer what he called the eternal spirit, that is, what makes his work valuable for all time. He prized Plato, Shakespeare, and Goethe above others; and gave the next place to Homer, Dante, and Swedenborg. He gave Carlyle a very high rank: considered his history of Frederick the Second even better than Thucydides. During the last year of his life, when he had almost lost his memory for names and people, he said to a visitor who called on him, "I have lately been reading a most interesting book about—" he hesitated for some time, "the greatest man that has lived for more than two centuries." Then he walked across the room and pointing to a long row of books added, "About that man." His friend looked and saw it was an edition of Goethe's forty volumes. Grimm's lectures on Goethe had lately been published.

The colored students of Howard University requested Emerson to give them a conversation on books, and tell them what they had better read; and he, remembering his own maxim, that the greatest prudence lies in concentration, limited himself purposely to a very few. He recommended Shakespeare and Milton of course; Gibbon's "Decline and Fall"; Boswell's "Life of Johnson"; Goethe's conversations with Eckermann and Goethe's autobiography. "Faust" he spoke of in rather a slighting manner; he did not think it possessed the eternal spirit. That so much of a puritan as Emerson should have admired Goethe is as remarkable as Goethe's admiration for so stanch an old puritan as Milton. The English writers of his own time, with the exception of Carlyle and possibly Tennyson, he did not like. He met Macaulay at one of Lady Holland's celebrated show dinners, and conceived a decided aversion for him. Such severely critical writers as Froude, Ruskin, and Matthew Arnold he never could like. He once had an interview with Ruskin, but it did not prove to be satisfactory. They differed on all points, and Ruskin complained that Emerson did not understand him. Six months afterwards Emerson remarked with his most amiable smile, "I expect Mr. Ruskin is still miserable because I could not understand him." But Ruskin's province lay outside of Emerson's, who cared little either for painting, sculpture, or music, or even for literature considered as an art. He had in his study a copy of Giotto's portrait of Dante which he evidently prized; and also Raphael Morghen's engraving of Guido's Aurora: but these were presents from his friends, and it is doubtful if he ever purchased a picture himself.

He was a frequent visitor at the Boston Athenaeum, and seized upon every new book of value as soon as it appeared: was the first to read translations of the Zendavesta and Confucius. He read almost every readable book in the English language as well as translations from all languages. He said he would as soon think of swimming across Charles River when he might make use of a bridge as to read a foreign book in the original if he could obtain a good translation.

This statement contains a good deal of truth, though it has been often traversed by those who learn languages easily and think because they get the literal meaning of Tacitus or Rousseau that they know all about the matter. The full significance, however, of any good writer can only be obtained by reflecting while we read, and the continuous exertion required to decipher a foreign tongue interferes with this not a little. If the reader can think in the language before him well and good, but few are so fortunate; and of those few not more than one in ten will be able to think in three or four different languages. Any person who has merely a conversational knowledge of Italian, for instance, would do much better to read the excellent translation we now have of Machiavelli than to read the original; and no one except a Greek professor would think of stumbling over Thucydides instead of using Jowett's version of it. So it is with Taine's "English Literature" and Von Hoist's history of American politics. On the other hand it may be said that no translation of the "Odes" of Horace has any value at all; and a faithful study of one book of the "Iliad" is worth all the translations from Homer that have ever been made. But the subject is an extensive one.

The tendency of pure democracy to Caesarism or imperialism has often been noticed, and the frequent change from one to the other has now become an established historical fact. Of this principle there is a curious illustration in Emerson's political opinions. He was in theory a pure democratist, but he would now and then make a remark which showed that he also believed in the rule of the strong hand. In his prose writings may be found two distinct lines of political thought emanating from these opposite views. He wrote a poem on Cromwell, and an essay on Napoleon, and evidently admired them both. In his "Boston Hymn" and in several other poems he comes very close to socialism. In "Woodnotes" he says:

"The lord is the peasant that was;
The peasant the lord that shall be,
The lord is the hay, the peasant the grass;
One dry, and one the living tree."

Democracy is limited in America by the conservative structure of our government and the good sense of the community. During Jackson's administration we came rather close to pure democracy, and nearly as close also to absolute despotism. Emerson was far from knowing this, but he felt that something was wrong. He wrote to Carlyle, "We have a most unfit man for President." On another occasion he wrote, "Politics are now in such a condition that the best principles are in one party, and the best men in the other." He appears to have voted with the best men. Again he would say, "If we can only once get the best man at the head of affairs we should be only too glad to turn everything over to him." Emerson, however, did not allow these theories to affect his practice. He always voted the whig ticket till 1844, and after that the free-soil and republican tickets.

It was the same with his doctrine of living according to nature. He never thought of doing this himself, except so far as a sensible mode of life and unaffected behavior may be considered so. He was the most conventional man in Concord, and as scrupulous of etiquette as an English clergyman. He was oftener seen with a silk-hat—what Mr. Howells calls a cylinder-hat—than any other person in the town. In his later years he declined to wear a wig, because it was not according to nature; but neither had he formerly worn a beard, which was quite as little according to nature.

In his earlier writings he celebrates the advantages of living in the country, but at sixty he concludes that the city is after all the best, if one has sufficient means,—especially for women, who require a current of human life to keep their minds healthy and cheerful. This reminds one of

Thorwaldsen's four seasons; in which spring and summer are represented by an out-of-door life, in autumn the corner of a house appears, and winter is wholly within doors. We expect a certain change of opinion in the course of years: it is the sign of a veracious character. Neither is it inconsistent for a practical man to sometimes deviate from the rules he has laid down for himself.

Emerson's real fault, if he may be said to have had one, was his optimism. Because he had been born with genius and was otherwise fortunate he thought every one else might succeed as easily as he had. In this way he often did people great injustice. If they were unfortunate he concluded that it must be their own fault. "Wherever there is failure," he said, "there is some giddiness, some lack of adaptation of means to ends." If he heard of anyone who could not obtain work he would say there is always plenty to do for willing hands. Those who were incapacitated by nature from earning their own living fared no better. He thought there was something which every one could do better than anybody else—which might possibly be true if there were as many professions as individuals. When some one spoke of a young German poet, whom it was thought but for his untimely death might have been the rival of Schiller, he said, "Yes, but he died: that was against him."

This line of thought logically resulted also in a kind of pessimism. He seemed at times to despise human nature. Somewhere about 1860 he wrote to a friend, "There is not one man in twenty that is worth the ground he stands on"; and speaking of Napoleon he affirms that, in the well-nigh universal negligence and inefficiency of mankind, we cannot be too thankful for this prompt and ready actor. No one who realizes the hard and bitter struggle for daily bread with which three-fourths of the human race are constantly occupied, would have written such a sentence. The transition from optimism to pessimism is very much like that from democracy to imperialism. [Footnote: The peculiar type of Emerson's optimism is illustrated in his poem called "Sea Shore" where he makes a fine catalogue of the gifts and advantages which the ocean brings to mankind, but says nothing of the terrible destructive power of the sea. He forgot that his old friend the Greek represented Neptune as even more cruel than the god of war. Did this man of heroic nature lack the courage to face tragedy?]

We regret to see him deciding the discovery of etherization in favor of his brother-in-law, Dr. Jackson; a question which a Congressional committee found itself unable to determine.

He had one trait of character which his biographers have not mentioned, and which might pass by the name of incredulity. He was the most difficult of men to persuade of any strange and remarkable event. Neither did he take the least pains to conceal his disbelief; and when you were telling him the living truth this was rather difficult to bear. When we said that a woodpecker had been seen in Walden woods nearly as large as a crow and quite as black, he shook his head and looked up at the pine trees. That was not according to his idea of a woodpecker. Neither did he like to hear anything which tended to prove the depravity of human nature. Stories of fraud and corruption in commercial or political life were not pleasant to his ears; and if the perpetrators escaped punishment he was evidently much annoyed. He liked to tell the truth better than he did to hear it.

When nearly sixty years of age both Emerson and Alcott fell in love with a charming young school-teacher of the transcendental sort, and it is rather pleasant to think that there was so much human nature still left in those grave old philosophers.

He was the most famous American of his time; not so celebrated perhaps in his own country as President Lincoln, but in foreign countries he surpassed all others,—such is the deep impression which a great writer makes on the minds of men. In Europe he was looked upon as the best representative of our Western Hemisphere. Carlyle celebrated him in England, and Grimm in Germany. The latter said, "There is no other living writer to whom I feel that I owe so much."

He had no public receptions in foreign cities, but everywhere the finest people united to honor him. On his second visit to England he complained that his time was almost consumed in answering letters of invitation. An English guest at the Harvard Phi Beta Kappa dinner said that when he returned home he would be asked two questions,—if he had seen Niagara Falls, and if he had met Emerson. He was a particular favorite with the English nobility, and whenever we saw a glittering carriage rolling down Concord turn-pike we felt sure it contained some earl or viscount who was paying his compliments to the poet of the pines. Emerson liked to entertain these distinguished visitors in his modest little parlor, but he never slighted his old friends for them; for he lived the wisdom that he taught, and the final virtue of this man was the religious humility of his nature.

MATTHEW ARNOLD'S LECTURE

During the earlier part of Emerson's career his religious philosophy met with such decided opposition that his friends were, very properly, all the more enthusiastic in his defence; and when the tide turned in his favor, and his fame rose continually higher and higher, the enthusiasm of his admirers reached a climax, and, like Webster before him, he became a veritable subject of idolization. His opponents, finding the current too strong for them, retreated into smooth water, waiting, like a defeated political party, for a favorable change of the tide. When, therefore, Matthew Arnold came to America in the autumn of 1883 expressly to lecture on Emerson, as a writer and thinker, there was great expectation on both sides, and both were equally disappointed. His friends who knew that he liked Emerson, thought he had found too much fault with him, and the other party considered he had praised him too highly.

Few men have ever done so much good in England as Matthew Arnold. Somewhere about the year 1830 Goethe remarked, that Englishmen, as such, were without reflection; party politics and the interests of trade interfered to prevent it; but they were great as practical men. This continued to be the order of the day, in spite of an occasional warning from Macaulay, for thirty years more, until finally Matthew Arnold came forward and said, "Do not be blinded any longer by the prejudices of self-interest, but endeavor to see things as they actually are." This was the continual chant of his life, repeated in a hundred different forms. He made use of the popularity he had gained by his fine, classic poetry, to teach his countrymen a lesson in culture. [Footnote: Lowell also made an excellent point when he warned Englishmen, at the Coleridge memorial, that if they were to regain the intellectual altitude of their ancestors, they must give up the adoration of common-sense, and pay more respect to imagination and ideality.]

Never did Demosthenes expose their faults to the Athenians more frankly and fearlessly, and with such manliness that at the time of his death there was no person in the British Islands more generally respected. On a trial vote that was taken by a London newspaper for membership to a proposed British Academy, Gladstone received the largest number of ballots, Tennyson the next and Matthew Arnold came third. He was considered the best literary critic in England, and if he had outlived Tennyson he would have succeeded him as laureate. He showed a dignified reserve in only publishing a very few books. Two small volumes of poetry, his "Essays in Criticism", which has become a standard work, and his American essays, are all that I know of. For all that, few writers were more celebrated in his own time, and it may be said that he fully deserved his monument in Westminster Abbey.

However, it must be admitted that as a critic he had certain peculiarities. He was, perhaps, too sensitive and impressible; too easily thrown off his guard by qualities in a writer for which he had an aversion. He would not only mention them once, but again and again. He ignored Schiller, who was at least one of the world's greatest dramatists; he was dissatisfied with Tennyson and could not endure Shelley at all. His attack on Francis Newman's translation of the "Iliad" was so severe that he finally discovered the fact himself. His preference for the classic style in literature was rather too decided; for we must never forget that Shakespeare himself was chiefly romantic. He liked poetry which was like his own, and seems to have unconsciously judged other poets by that standard. He had no patience with idiomatic writing like that of Carlyle or Jean Paul; and he made incessant warfare on the subjective method. It is true that subjectivity may be called the peculiar vice of the nineteenth century, and yet it is a vice like the self-consciousness of the early Christians, that ought finally to end in virtue. There are thousands of readers whose minds cannot be reached in any other way.

Allowances must sometimes be made also for the physical condition of a writer. Not always; for Carlyle wrote the greatest of dramatic histories while he was suffering from dyspepsia in the most distressing manner. However, I think in Matthew Arnold's case something may be conceded to him. He came to lecture in America for a double purpose—to tell the truth and to repair his fortunes. It was a sad story. His son had failed in business; his father, of course, had endorsed his notes, and he found himself at the threshold of old age as poor as in the beginning. Such a shock is felt severely enough by tough, hard-fisted men of the world, but to the tender sensibility of a poet it must have been a crushing blow. There can be as little doubt that it brought on the malady that abbreviated his life, as that it gave a melancholic tone to his thought and filled his mind with gloomy forebodings.

The opening of his address was very beautiful. He recalls the impression made upon him in his youth by the writing of Carlyle, Goethe, Emerson and Francis Newman, and says:

"Forty years ago, when I was an undergraduate at Oxford, voices were in the air which haunt my memory still. Happy the man who in that susceptible season of youth hears such voices! they are a possession to him forever. No such voices are there now. Oxford has more criticism now, more knowledge, more light; but such voices as those of our youth it has no longer. The name of Cardinal Newman is a great name to the imagination still; his genius and his style are things of power..... A greater voice still,—the greatest voice of the century,—came to us in those youthful years through Carlyle: the voice of Goethe. To this day,—such is the force of youthful associations,—I read his 'Wilhelm Meister' with more pleasure in Carlyle's translation than in the original. The large, liberal view of human life in 'Wilhelm Meister,' how novel it was to the Englishman in those days! and it was salutary, too, and educative for him, doubtless, as well as novel..... And besides those voices, there came to us in that old Oxford time a voice also from this side of the Atlantic,—a clear and pure voice, which for my ear, at any rate, brought a strain as new, and moving, and unforgettable, as the strain of Newman, or Carlyle, or Goethe.... He was your Newman, your man of soul and genius visible to you in the flesh, speaking to your bodily ears, a present object for your heart and imagination. That is surely the most potent of all influences!"

I confess I enjoy these clear classic sentences so full of tenderness, and yet with the latent fire of manhood in them, much better than Emerson's weird, concentrated epigrams, wonderful as those sometimes are. Comparatively speaking it is like the difference between a living elm and oak timber. But the writer does not long maintain this elevated tone. He soon becomes despondent, and his glorious sunrise, like that in Shakespeare's sonnet, is lost to him again.

"For out alack, he was but one hour mine;
The region cloud hath veiled him from me now."

He remembers that Francis Newman is now Cardinal Newman; that Carlyle's career had ended with his furious "Latter-day Pamphlets," and even in Emerson he had found a certain kind of disappointment.

Yet there may be a deeper reason in this;—the reason that sometimes underlies a coincidence. We too in early life were strengthened and filled with enthusiasm by the earnest voice of Emerson, the trenchant eloquence of Wendell Phillips, and the brilliant wit and penetrating humor of Lowell; but the public activity of Emerson soon afterwards ceased; Phillips became a socialist and ultimately a demagogue; while Lowell changed his verses for foreign missions and after-dinner speeches. There is a prevalent feeling that the nineteenth century, which was ushered in to the sound of Napoleon's cannon and is now going rather tamely out in a discussion of the laws of economics, has not more than half accomplished the work that was assigned it. There is everywhere among thinking men a feeling of distrust and half disappointment. Lowell felt it here, George Eliot in England; and Herman Grimm in Germany, a sanguine man, speaks of the deep-seated unrest which almost drives us to despair.

As I turn from my desk to the morning's newspaper I find in it the following extract from one of Emerson's earlier essays:

"Trust the time. What a fatal prodigality to condemn our age—we cannot overvalue it—it is our all. As the wandering sea-bird which, crossing the ocean, alights on some rock or islet to rest for a moment its wings, and to look back on the wilderness of waves behind, and onward to the wilderness of waters before—so stand we perched on this rock or shoal of time, arrived out of the immensity of the past, bound and road-ready to plunge into immensity again. Not for nothing it dawns out of everlasting peace, this great discontent, this self-accusing reflection. The very time sees for us, thinks for us. It is a microscope such as philosophy never had. Insight is for us which was never for any, and doubt not, the moment and the opportunity are divine. Wondering we come into this lodge of watchmen, this office of espial; let us not retreat astonished and ashamed. Let us go out of the hall door, and doubt never but a good genius brought us in and will carry us out."

Now this is a prose poem, so beautiful that it seems hardly to need the help of rhyme and metre to make it sing; and, as high art always must, it covers a profound truth,—truth that lies at the foundation of all tragedy,—namely, that we are obliged to trust time though time destroys us; that we must trust our fellow men though they often deceive us; that we must trust the ground we stand on though the earthquake devour us.

But Emerson does not say this, and I doubt if he anywhere says it. He was too much of an optimist to perceive it. He wished all the stories he read to turn out fortunately, and if they did not so much the worse for them. Gladstone is the same kind of a man. He believes that the right will always finally conquer; and so it may when the day of judgment arrives and the affairs of the universe are at last wound up. It gives him, as it did Emerson, a tremendous energy,—almost like fanaticism, but it must in the nature of things affect his political judgment. The lives of these two stretch nearly across the nineteenth century, and their popularity is evidence that they represent their own time better than most others.

What does Emerson intend by trusting the time? Does he mean the spirit of the age? If we replace the word time by Divine Providence, the passage becomes intelligible and notably significant; but if he meant the prevailing spirit of the time, the earlier part of Emerson's career is a perfect contradiction of it. If in his youth he had trusted the prevailing tendency of his time he would have become a conservative formalist, and never heard of as an independent thinker. It might even be said that few men have ever trusted their own time less. Like Gladstone, he was dissatisfied with the present and looked toward the future. They both exerted themselves with all their might to revolutionize public opinion and give to the future the stamp of their own ideas. The old Hebrew prophets whom Emerson so much resembled did not trust their own time, but were constantly complaining of it. So Cicero cried out, "O tempora, O mores!" and Savonarola, and many others.

It would seem as if in this poetic rhapsody the writer had lost sight of his subject almost immediately upon stating it, and had substituted Providence for it in his mind. This was not unfrequently the case with him, and may account for those vague aerial flights which his commentators have referred to. Hawthorne says, "Mr. Emerson is a great searcher for facts, but they seem to melt away and become unsubstantial in his grasp." However, it was not facts but ideas that he was in quest of.

The whole of Matthew Arnold's essay is thoughtful and interesting, but it has one grand defect. After saying that Emerson's writings constituted the most important prose work of the nineteenth century, he fails to support the statement by sufficient arguments. If he had developed this point to such a length as its importance deserved, and then finished his discourse with a glowing tribute to Emerson as a man, his audience might have found slight cause to complain of him; but after simply stating the fact, he proceeded to a lengthy discussion of Emerson's stoical philosophy, and finally branched off on a criticism of Carlyle and the consideration of happiness as the true end of life. We will only pause here to remark that the true end of life does not seem to us to be happiness so much as development, and the evolution of such characters as Emerson and Matthew Arnold.

His condemnation of Emerson's poetry was a still severer blow. Emerson's friends had endured enough already on that score. Nothing was ever made so much fun of by parodists and other small wits. In any social company, if Emerson's poetry was mentioned somebody was sure to raise a laugh; and there was nothing that could be done about it. It was hoped that Matthew Arnold's prestige would put a final end to this nonsense, which was nothing but a fashionable habit; but he added the weight of his position as professor of literature to the other side of the scale. He praised certain portions very highly, but averred that these were exceptional, and concluded with what seems to be a "reductio ad absurdum," namely, that Longfellow's poem of "The Bridge" or Whittier's "School Days" was worth the whole body of Emerson's verse. As these were anything but the best of Longfellow and Whittier it seemed rather inconsistent in Matthew Arnold to have praised Emerson's poetry at all; and this was the more surprising after his courageous defence of Wadsworth a short time before. Those who like Emerson's poetry usually like Wordsworth's and *vice versa*.

But Emerson's poetry is a peculiar subject. Carlyle and Lowell, both eminent critics, did not condemn it, but at the same time they were slow to praise it. Dr. F. H. Hedge, who probably knew more about literature than either of them, considered it poetry of a very high order, and Rev. William Furness of Philadelphia, when some one spoke slightingly of Emerson as a poet, exclaimed, "He is heaven high above our other poets!" In many obituary notices at the time of his death, he was mentioned as being easily the first of American poets. Professor Tyndall has a great admiration for his poetry; and so has another professor we know of whom we will not mention, but who is an equally good chemist. Dr. O. W. Holmes' life of Emerson was dreaded by many for fear of the position he might assume on this question, but to the general surprise of the public, he took strong grounds in favor of it; so that since that time, whenever people laugh at Emerson's poetry it is only necessary to ask them if they have read Dr. Holmes' biography of him.

Immediately after the lecture, a lively discussion began about it in the newspapers, in which leading writers, scholars and professors took an active part. How much soever they might disagree in regard to Emerson, they all united in a disapproval of the lecturer's estimate of him. Matthew Arnold did not seem to have a partisan in the country. The discussion was renewed a year later when his book of discourses in America was published, and then David A. Wasson wrote the following letter which was published in the "Christian Register":

ARNOLD ON EMERSON

"It may be doubted whether Matthew Arnold's critical estimate of Emerson as a prose writer is well understood by most of those who take it in ill part. The judgment expressed is that Emerson is the pre-eminent prose writer of his century, not as being either a great philosopher or great in his style of workmanship, but for the reason that he is a great spiritual light, the purest, whitest, serenest, of a century now drawing toward its close. This taken together is valuable praise, and converted into disparagement by its denial to Emerson of two special distinctions; and in respect to both, the denial is taken, I think, to cover much more ground than it was intended to cover. To keep within the limits, I will here attend to but one of these, where it must be confessed, Mr. Arnold is himself to blame for the misconstruction put upon him, since he has expressed himself in a way to facilitate, if not to invite, such a mistake. Emerson, it is said, was the most important writer of this century, yet was not a great writer. How should this be, unless, indeed, the century as a whole is inferior, and prominence in it is no token of greatness? In truth, Mr. Arnold has used the term 'writer' in two widely different senses. In the one use it refers to the content of the writing, to its intellectual and moral import, its spiritual significance; in the other use it refers to the writing itself considered as showing more or less of literary power,—that is, of power in the ordering and verbal embodiment of thoughts and conceptions.

"Declining to be misled by this ambiguity, let us inquire what is meant, when it is said that Emerson was not a great writer. To my apprehension the meaning is simply that his literary execution, taken by and for itself, was not of the highest order. A cotton fabric may be better woven than one of silk, a chain of copper be better wrought and linked than a chain of gold. He that should recognize the better workmanship where it exists would not thereby set the cheaper material above the more precious, for he would not institute a comparison to any effect whatsoever between the two. Nor would he betray a shallow and petty mind, as making much of things trivial. Mr. Arnold says of Emerson's writings, the matter is gold, but the workmanship does not evince the highest skill. Were this last urged as determining the value of the writer we might indeed say that the critic offends by exalting a subordinate distinction to the first place. But it is not so urged, nor is there anything to indicate that Mr. Arnold makes perfection of literary execution the be-all and end-all of excellence in literature; indeed one does not see that he at all exaggerates its importance. Those whom he mentions as great writers were for the most part second-rate men—second-rate men that is as measured by the standard of the ages; and it does not appear that he thinks of them otherwise than as such. Cicero receives the title while it is not given to Marcus Antoninus; but it is sufficiently apparent that Mr. Arnold sets a higher value upon Marcus Antoninus than upon Cicero. Voltaire is one of the great writers; but in the world's literature he is at best but first among the lesser lights, and there is no sign that Matthew Arnold attributed to him a higher importance. Or take the case of Swift. The literary talents of this unhappy man were indeed prodigious: he performed feats to which we cannot say that any other would have been equal: he is as unique as Shakespeare,—though, of course, in a vastly lower way. But did he contribute one great thought or one grand and salutary imagination to the world's stock? Not to my knowledge. Did he shed light upon any important province of human interest, upon religion, morals, politics, art, science, history, education, manners or whatever else? I cannot report that he did so. Did he lay a noble emphasis upon any great truth or order of truths and so recommend it effectually to the attention and consideration of mankind? Or did he even write a single sentence which one treasures up as an imperishable jewel? In fine, does his work serve to enlarge the souls, enlighten the minds, direct the wills or quicken and inspire the better powers of man? Does it so much as breathe upon them a salubrious air? Alas no! To all such questions the answer, or mine own at least, will be negative. Yet he was indeed a great writer: that is, he had a great, a truly wonderful power of conception and representation. Mr. Arnold, who for aught one can discover to the contrary, distinguishes the nature of Swift's genius and prizes it only for what it is worth, does not claim that Emerson was a greater writer in the same sense, but thinks his deliverance somewhat faulty, especially as wanting that continuity which belongs to good literary tissue, as to every other.

"Suppose him quite wrong in this, still the error is not one to be warm about, since it leaves the Concord essayist in his place of pre-eminence, and is put forth only by way of determining the kind of value which shall be attributed to his writings.

"D. A. Wasson."

This was forwarded to Matthew Arnold, who was then at his own home, and in due time this reply was received from him:

"COBHAM, SURREY,

"Jan. 7th., 1886.
"Dear Sir,

"I have just had, on my return to England, your letter and Mr. Wasson's paper, and must thank you for them.

"Very much of what Mr. Wasson says is true; yet literary style is more than he makes it—the mere dressing up of a material which may be inferior; it is itself in the material and has an extraordinary value. No great writer is to be disposed of as Mr. Wasson disposes of Addison and Swift; he says, nothing is to be learned from Swift; why, a sense for the blatant nonsense and claptrap which constitutes three-fourths of our public writing and speaking, and which is a greater curse to your country that even to ours, is to be got from him. Addison has his valuable criticism of life too; I doubt whether to a Taine, a hundred years hence, he will not seem of more importance than Emerson, who was above all things of value in his own day. But I love Emerson.

"Truly yours,

"Matthew Arnold."

Taine, who preferred Macaulay to Carlyle, might also prefer Addison to Emerson; but it is not likely that a future Grimm or another Sainte-Beuve would do so. In his "Essays in Criticism," Matthew Arnold enters a general complaint against English prose writers for a lack of mental flexibility, and against Addison particularly for the commonplaceness of his ideas. He was a severe and exacting critic.

DAVID A. WASSON

Bryant, Longfellow, Emerson, Hawthorne and Whittier were all nearly of the same age, and formed a literary galaxy such as has been rare enough in any country or period of history. They are distinguished, however, by one peculiarity—a slight sentimentalism which belonged to the time in which they grew up, and is most strongly marked in Longfellow and least so in Hawthorne. Fifteen or twenty years later there appeared, as usually happens, a number of talented imitators or admirers, and with them two men of equal genius who may be looked upon as the corrective and antidote for their predecessors. These were James Russell Lowell and David Atwood Wasson.

They were as different as Goldsmith and Dr. Johnson. Lowell was a fine poet, a humorist and man of the world. He wrote easily and lived easily. He was the companion of wealthy and distinguished men. He acquired prosperity, as it were, by natural inclination. Next to the King of Prussia he was the most fortunate man of his time. He knew something of sorrow, but of hardship and misfortune only by hearsay. He was the child of summer, and revelled in it; but this continual happiness brought with it certain limitations. Though he was a veracious man, he was rarely a serious one. He never became thoroughly in earnest until he was stimulated by partisan feeling. His best poems were inspired by the anti-slavery conflict, and the rendition of Mason and Slidell; and it was just on these occasions that his humor was most brilliant and pleasant flavored. His productiveness was not great, and his other writings do not make a strong impression. It is said that he often tried to write a book, but was never able to concentrate himself on one subject for a sufficient length of time. He is easily the first of American humorists. The greatest compliment ever paid Thoreau was that such a man as Lowell could not understand him.

Wasson must have been born under the constellation of the Little Bear. As the Germans say, his life was always winter. Every possible obstacle was placed in his way, and misfortune came to him at one time or another in almost every shape. The difficulties he encountered in life were too great for him, and prevented the full fruition of his genius. The wonder is that they did not crush him altogether. He never acquired the sufficient public influence nor received the recognition his merit deserved. He was by nature a thinker—a seeker after truth. There was no problem,—social, political or philosophical,—which he was not ready to grapple with. He could plunge into these subjects like a pearl-diver who means to touch bottom, and would never come out till his last breath was spent. This mental habit and his continual suffering made him only too serious, too much in earnest. Jests were not in his line, but he sometimes wrote poetry of the very highest order. He is the first and most original of American thinkers.

What these two dissimilar men had in common was good Anglo-Saxon manliness—which is after all the foundation of common-sense. They wished to live as other men had lived before them, and not in any new, unusual, or eccentric manner. They believed that virtue was to be found in the great world rather than out of it; among human habitations, and in dealing with all kinds of people rather than by an isolated life at Brook Farm or in Walden Woods. They sought not after any rare and Utopian excellencies, but contented themselves with a plain, sensible, every-day morality. They were neither vegetarians, teetotalers, non-resistants, nor socialists. They considered it no sin to love a woman or to fight a man. They may be called anti-sentimentalists.

Neither were they blind followers of custom and tradition. They wished to be in the vanguard of civilization, and they were conscious that to do this they must not only accept the results of others, but add something of their own. They endeavored to become acquainted with the best that was thought and known in their time, both in literature and in other matters. They thus became excellent critics, as well as versatile and many-sided men. They were among the most cultivated men of the century, and are the most cosmopolitan of American writers. That they should not have possessed greater influence was largely owing to the tendencies of their time. The current of the age was too strong for them, and in their later years they both expressed gloomy forebodings of the future, both for their own country and the rest of the civilized world.

Wasson went to Concord in 1859 intending to make it his permanent abode, but the offer of a philanthropic gentleman who wished to take him into his own house for a year and care for him, as Mr. Badams of Manchester entertained Carlyle, induced him to emigrate again. He continued however in friendly communication with the literary people there, often visited them, and now lies buried in Sleepy Hollow cemetery, so that he deserves to be classed among them, rather than with any other group of literary men.

He was born in Brooksville, Maine, on the fourteenth of May, 1823. He was named David for his father, and Atwood for Miss Harriet Atwood, a female preacher and missionary who was at that time his mother's devoted friend,—and it has been said that Wasson attributed his unusual mental activity largely to her influence. His mother died while he was still too young to recollect her, but her place was fortunately supplied by a kindly and sensible stepmother; not such a rare phenomenon as some people think. His father belonged to a class of men only to be found on the coast of Maine, who are at once fishermen, farmers and navigators; a much more intelligent and cultivated class than the agricultural people of the interior. It is a beautiful sail among the islands from Rockland to Mount Desert, and the pleasantest part of it, to me at least, is the sight of the well kept farms with their handsome cattle and clean-shaven hay-fields, which line the coast. Our best ship-builders have originated among these people.

Brooksville is a thinly scattered settlement on the westerly side of a rocky and even mountainous peninsula. A deep and narrow strait separates it from Castine, which has to be crossed in a ferry-boat. The house of David Wasson, Senior, is something more than half-a-mile from the ferry landing; a large, commodious, two-story house, much better than the average of farm-houses, with two large barns and numerous out-buildings. Between it and the street is an orchard, and on one side a latticed porch or piazza. West of it there is a trout-brook and beyond that a hemlock grove, and the blue hills of Camden in the distance. On the south side the sea comes up to the edge of the farm, and the road to Sedgwick winds about the ridge on the East. It was a fitting birthplace for a poet or a painter.

He has left us a valuable and quite unique sketch of his early boyhood, [Footnote: Essays, Religious, Social, Political. D. A. Wasson. Boston: Lee and Shepard.] in which he confesses to having been a sensitive, excitable and passionate little fellow such as the more cool-headed and phlegmatic sort could tease and worry at pleasure. Since he was also very high-spirited, this resulted inevitably in a good many fights, and from being naturally peaceable and tender-hearted he became at last the most noted pugilist in that community. It is said that at seventeen he could smash a door-panel with his fist. That he disliked work on the farm is not surprising. Manual labor is injurious to boys physically and mentally; and they should be saved from it, except perhaps in the haying or harvesting seasons, as much as possible. Otherwise he was modest, orderly, truthful, and the finest scholar that had ever been known about Castine. His father recognized his superior abilities, and made an effort to send him to Bowdoin College.

There were many obstacles in the way, however, and he did not enter until 1845. He never told me much about his college life. He was older than his companions and more serious. The light spirit that makes it a joyous festival to many was not in him. Of the myrtle and ivy of sweet two-

and-twenty he knew nothing. He distinguished himself in mathematics (especially in geometry, which is the most logical of studies) and in the students' debating-societies. He was also an excellent gymnast.

In almost every college class there are a number of over-grown boys who had better have been sent to the reform-school. On the occasion of a class supper, or some such celebration, young Wasson saved half-a-dozen of these roaring blades from disgrace and suspension, by his timely interference. It was already far into the night, and being fairly intoxicated, they took it into their minds to return and attend morning prayers in the college chapel. In order to prevent this catastrophe, Wasson arranged a bowling match for a fictitious sum of money with the most sober man he could find, and in that way delayed the party until the dangerous hour had passed. It was supposed to have been some of the same set who the following autumn set fire to and consumed the college wood-pile—a severe loss, and a dangerous precedent. No trace of the incendiaries could be discovered and the college faculty suspended on suspicion right and left. Among those whom the lightning struck were several that Wasson knew or felt sure could have had nothing to do with it; and he accordingly went to the president and argued the case with him. This resulted in his being summoned before the next faculty meeting. When asked whether he knew who the perpetrators of the outrage were, he declined to answer, not because he had positive knowledge but because he felt morally certain in regard to them. A few weeks later, after he had gone into the country to teach school for the winter, he received word that he had been suspended. Indignant at what he considered an injustice to his character and scholarship, he left Bowdoin forever: nor did he perhaps lose much by this. The philosophical studies of the senior year could be mastered as easily by a mind like Wasson's without an instructor as with one. He never studied for rank and cared little or nothing for college honors or degrees.

There is no good art without a sense of delicacy; and this mental delicacy is usually matched by some kind of physical sensitiveness. Artists are, according to the vulgar phrase, more thin-skinned than other people. Both at Bowdoin College, and afterwards while at the divinity-school, Wasson worked hard in summer and taught school in winter so as to help in defraying the expense of his education. In this mode of life he encountered many hardships that were too severe for him. I notice among my own classmates that very few of those who lived in this manner reached the age of thirty-five. The food which Wasson encountered during his winter peregrinations was anything but what human beings are intended to eat. On one occasion he returned from his school to dine as usual in a cold room, and found himself provided there with the skeleton of a chicken, two large beets, a pie made of preserved barberries, and biscuits which pulled out when separated, like a telescope. The meat, unless fried, was always cooked too much; bread and vegetables insufficiently. Like many another young hero he believed in facing these obstacles, and overcoming them by main force. A strain which he received in a wrestling match during the celebrated Tippecanoe campaign may have done him harm; but a more serious injury was incurred while on a trip to Bangor in one of his father's schooners the summer after he was suspended from college. The captain of the schooner appears to have been a sea-faring brute who had a secret grudge, a sort of town-and-gown feeling, against the scholar, and was ready to do him any mischief he could. They were to take on a cargo of lumber at Bangor and the captain requested Wasson, who was not actually under his orders, to stow it away in the hold while two men on deck handed the boards to him as fast as possible. Wasson felt that something was wrong and might have protested against it, but his youthful pride, and perhaps a feeling of indifference in regard to his fate, prevented him. I believe he finally fainted from over-exertion and the close air, and was never a well man again. The trouble was not very bad at first, and might easily have been cured by suitable treatment, and a quiet, methodical life: but there was no doctor in that part of Maine who could prescribe properly for him. He tried some short sea-voyages, but these did him little good. So Prescott injured his eyesight through the same proud spirit; but it was this pride which made him afterwards what he was.

His ill-health however did not prevent him from studying and writing. The following autumn he went into the office of a lawyer and member of Congress in Castine and read "Blackstone," "Chitty on Bills," and some other law-books. The study of law is in itself an excellent nerve tonic, balancing the mind and strengthening the character. Nothing could have been better for him at this juncture, and it is an unlimited pity that he did not continue it longer. But the law could never have satisfied the aspirations of his nature any more than Columbus might have been satisfied with sailing a packet in the Mediterranean. He liked the study of it, and once spoke with great respect of "Chitty on Bills" wishing he could find a work on theology or politics that contains so much good sense; but he longed for something beyond it. The congressman had a good opinion of his abilities and held out the prospect of a partnership to him, but personal ambition was not an ingredient in Wasson's nature. He was discontented and ready for a change.

One day in June 1849 he was sent to a distant town on what was to his sensitive moral nature a most disgusting expedition; namely, to help a lucrative client take the poor debtor's oath, and so avoid a partially unjust debt. On his return home he stopped at a country store to make a small purchase, and there at the end of the shelf he saw a cheap dingy copy of

Carlyle's "Sartor Resartus." He purchased it, and read it in his wagon by the evening light. He had tried to read it before, but failed to make his way in it. It was the first clear message and sure token of a spiritual life that had yet reached him. He had lived through the "everlasting no," and here was the "everlasting yea" set plainly before him. Years afterward M. D. Conway told Carlyle of walking in the woods at Groveland with Wasson, and how his face became radiant with internal light when he spoke of "Sartor Resartus."

This new-birth from above seized upon him like a fever. He now felt that he had a mission in life; a message to mankind. And in what way could he deliver this message? How could he make known to others what was in his full heart, except from the pulpit? For the first time he conceived the ministry as a high-minded and ennobling profession. He decided accordingly to go into the church. His family were Calvinists, and Calvinism was the only mode of faith of which he knew very much. That such a step should have been inspired by the writings of a heretic like Carlyle was in itself a contradiction which foreboded an ultimate collision. Yet no man perhaps ever lived who had a clearer sense of a Divine Presence in the universe than Thomas Carlyle, and it was this which Wasson recognized in him. Poets and philosophers are naturally heretical, because they take the short road of genius which others find it difficult to follow. But all believers finally arrive at the same destination.

He entered the theological seminary at Bangor in 1849 and graduated in 1851. It may be he went there with a youthful idea of reforming the church. At any rate his boldness of thought and free utterance brought him into suspicion with his fellow students, and at one time reports were in circulation that he was to be expelled for heresy. With his customary directness he went to the president, Dr. Pond, and inquired if there was any truth in this. The doctor, who really liked Wasson, received him with a kindly, patriarchal manner and said: "Do not be troubled, my young friend, we all have our seasons of doubt. I have had mine; but take my word for it that it is all right. For look at those saints up there in glory. How did they get there?" Such an argument was not likely to relieve the fermentation in his mind. Walking the streets of Bangor at this time was Dr. Frederick Henry Hedge, the man of all others who might have solved Wasson's doubts in a satisfactory manner, and with whom Wasson afterwards found himself in more complete moral and intellectual sympathy than with any other of his friends. Wasson saw him frequently, but had no opportunity of making his acquaintance. So nearly do we either hit it, or miss it, all through life!

The only person who sympathized with him in his progressive views of religion was Miss Abbie Smith, the daughter of an apothecary in Newburyport, Massachusetts. She was visiting at the house of her brother who was one of the instructors at the Seminary. That he should have fallen in love with her, and soon become engaged to her is therefore not surprising. They were married the year after his graduation, and she continued a faithful, industrious and uncomplaining wife; his mainstay in ill-health and misfortune till the end. They were not always happy together; but it is a rare marriage where that is the case. Wasson's struggle with the world was often reflected in his own family, disturbing the harmony and comfort of it. His wife once said quite gravely, that there were others from whom her husband would probably have made a selection if he had not offered himself to her. He was always a favorite with the other sex, and equally fond of their society. As he never troubled himself much as to what people said of him, this gave rise to a good deal of talk which his opponents took advantage of to disparage his character. He was once a witness in a divorce case, and a rather tricky lawyer who had a remarkable faculty for what Bacon calls "turning the cat in the pan," succeeded in making him appear at a disadvantage; but Mrs. Wasson told me that he was in the right. If his wife had no suspicion of him we need have none.

He went directly from Bangor to Groveland, a pleasant village beautifully situated on the Merrimack, which from Haverhill to the sea is one of the finest American rivers. His *fiancee* had numerous relatives in the place, and it was owing to her influence that he received a call there. At first all the signs were favorable; the young minister was well liked, and his parishioners were only afraid that a man of such rare ability would soon gravitate to a larger congregation. So he might have done, if his ardent, aspiring soul would have permitted him to temporize with his conscience, and to be content with mere popularity and doing good on a small scale. But the thought that was matured within him could no longer be restrained. The dangerous seed sown by reading "Sartor Resartus" had now become a strong young tree and must have air and light or it would perish. In October 1852 he preached a sermon that fairly astounded his amiable parishioners. He argued that regeneration and salvation were not to be obtained by blind faith in Jesus, but by intelligent moral culture and spiritual development. This view was, as far as I know, original with Wasson, and should be distinguished from the anti-miraculous standpoint of Parker and the natural supernaturalism of Emerson. Almost at the same hour an English naturalist was applying the same principle to the origin of species, and the evolution of the human race from the lower animals. The Englishman's clear, inductive insight was matched by the philosophical penetration of an American. The Darwinian theory now stands uncontested among scientific men, and whether admitted or not there is quite as surely an evolution apparent in the history of religion, not very unlike it. This is the lesson of the nineteenth century.

The following day one of the deacons of the church called upon Wasson to inform him that his sermon had given offence and that he must retract from his position. "But," replied the minister, "I cannot! I am not going to retract it." Thirty years after this Wasson laughed as heartily, as a suffering person very well could, while he recollected the expression of astonishment on the worthy deacon's face. That a man should do wrong for the sake of money or some material advantage was conceivable to him—he had known instances of that; but that any man should so stand in his own light both for this world and the next, was a moral incongruity which he could not understand. Wasson would not withdraw from his position, but followed it up the next Sunday by a still more energetic statement. There was nothing left now but deposition. A conference was called and Wasson regularly expelled from the Congregational brotherhood. Even some Unitarians also shared in the horror. About a third part of his congregation, however, were converted by him and established an independent church; so that after all he achieved a kind of victory.

Wasson had now escaped in a two-fold sense from the fog-banks and shallow waters of his native coast and henceforward was to sail forth bravely upon the high seas. The conflict he had passed through attracted no little attention from thoughtful and cultivated people, and even those who did not wholly agree with him admired the honest manliness with which he defended his views. Polite society opened its doors to him. Wherever he went now he was received as a distinguished guest. He soon made the acquaintance of eminent scholars and men of letters,—of Sumner, Parker and Emerson. He made friends everywhere. He began to publish essays and poems; at first in the "Christian Examiner," and afterwards in the "Atlantic Monthly." In those days of plain living and high thinking it was not customary for magazine writers to sign their names, (so modest were they,) to their contributions; and in this way Wasson just missed the general celebrity which they might have brought him, but their merit was recognized by those of whose good opinion he was chiefly desirous.

The effort, however, had been too much for him. The only chance of recovery from a nervous disorder lies in freedom from mental agitation. An injured nerve requires a longer time to heal than a broken bone and quite as much care and self-denial. Any serious disturbance to the circulation produces a pressure in the blood vessels of the nervous centres, and tears away the improvement that has commenced there. Then nature has to begin her work over again; and if this happens repeatedly nature becomes tired of working in vain and refuses to give further assistance. This was Wasson's misfortune. He was sensitive and excitable by temperament, the injury to his spine had made him still more so, and the mental agitation he experienced during 1852 and 1853 was enough to prevent him from ever being restored to perfect health. During these two years he must have endured nothing less than the tortures of the inquisition; and no doubt some of his Calvinistic neighbors considered it a judgment on him for his heresy. A mutilated life is not so very bad after one is used to it, but the beginning is terrible. It is like being surrounded with invisible barbed fences, which we inevitably run against and lacerate ourselves with, until we learn to bear in mind their exact position. Accidents too happen to nervous invalids which other people seem generally to escape from. Wasson was at one time making fair progress in his condition when suddenly one day, as he was walking through Boston, the door of a house opened and a lady slipping on some ice and tripping over the steps fell right into his arms. This was a highly diverting adventure for a young clergyman, but it cost him weeks of suffering. A somewhat similar strain came upon him when his first child was born. He does not seem to have ever met with a physician who understood his case. One worthy doctor in Worcester invited him to his house and drove with him in his sulky for more than half a year, without accomplishing anything for him. He went on a voyage to London and another to Smyrna, without any better result than suffering from bad food and stormy weather. After the first voyage his condition was so bad that, as he said of it once, he scarcely knew whether it was day or night: but the climate of Asia Minor agreed with him and he returned from Smyrna at least better for so much experience. I think his first real improvement came during his stay at my father's house. There he had plentiful repose, both of mind and body, and if good medical treatment had been added he might have made a substantial gain.

In the spring of 1864 Bradford, the marine artist, being ambitious to paint icebergs in their native wilds, organized a sailing party for Labrador and invited Wasson to go with them. This was the first enterprise of the kind that gave him permanent benefit. Fortunately they encountered no severe storms. The cool, bracing air of the polar regions was better than galvanism and stimulated his nerves to work in the proper way. Sailing along the coast they were able to anchor almost every night in smooth water. The fish they caught, the strange birds they saw and stranger human creatures, were a cheerful entertainment to him. He became quite a sportsman, and even joined one day in the pursuit of a polar bear. He returned in the autumn practically cured of his trouble, but to regain his strength was out of the question: he suffered besides very badly from dyspepsia. However he was able to preach regularly, to make speeches in public, to work in his garden and write perhaps three hours a day. Such a person is not greatly to be pitied, and if he had fortunately possessed a small competency we might now look upon him as a prosperous man: but his only property consisted of a good working library and five hundred dollars which a friend had given him. The next eight years were the best and most productive of his life; and he might have continued in the same course but for another most unfortunate accident. The supply of coal in his government office gave out, and the requisition for a fresh quantity was not promptly filled. Wasson sat writing in a cold room. There was a sudden change of weather, a severe snow squall, and the result was—pleurisy. This changed to bronchitis which worried and weakened him for the following ten years, and finally carried him off in his sixty-fifth year. That he went through a severe fever at the house of his friend Henry A. Page of Medford is hardly worth considering, for he was so tenderly and beautifully cared for there as almost to make it an enviable experience; but in 1879 cataracts formed on both eyes, one of which had been injured long before, and when they were operated on, two years later, the sight was restored to his injured eye (such as it was previously) but not to the other, so that he was left very nearly blind. He attributed this catastrophe to the quantity of belladonna which had been prescribed for him.

Such was his pathological history and a truly terrible one it is. Who can remember the like of it? Certainly Job's trials were not heavier nor were they borne with more fortitude and patience. In the midst of his severest troubles he wrote "All is well:" a noble religious poem equal to the hymn of Cleanthes or the twelfth ode of Horace; and in one of his earlier essays he speaks of tragedy as possessing such beauty and grandeur that he is almost ready to believe it is the proper goal and destination of earthly life. In "Epic Philosophy" he says: "Strife is around man, and strife is within him; the lightning thrusts its blazing scymitar through his roof, the thief creeps in at his door, and remorse at his heart. Who, looking on these things, does not acknowledge that man is indeed fearfully as well as wonderfully made? Who would not sometimes cry, 'O that my eyes were a fountain of tears, that I might weep, not the desolations of Israel alone, but the hate of Israel to Edom and of Edom to Israel, the jar, the horror, the ensanguined passion and ferocity of Nature'? But when we would despair, behold we cannot. Out of the conscious heart of humanity issues forever, more or less clearly, a voice of infinite, pure content. 'Through the valley of the shadow of death I will fear no evil, for THOU art with me.' Sometimes, when our trial is sorest, that voice is clearest, singing as from the jaws of death and the gates of hell. And now, though the tears fall, they become jewels as they fall; and the sorrow that begot them wears them in the diadem of its more than regal felicity."

This is the echo of his own experience; the spiritual diagnosis of his case. With what fortitude he endured his maladies those who knew him best can bear witness. He was no ideal Stoic nor self-conscious martyr; but more like an Homeric hero fighting his troubles, bearing them bravely, talking of them sensibly, always glad to receive sympathy but never seeking it, and complaining when he could endure no longer. He never tried to comfort himself by sophistical reflections, but elevated thoughts were always his chief consolation. Conversation about great writers and thinkers always seemed to strengthen him.

Mr. Frothingham in his excellent memoir speaks of Wasson as a self-consuming nature. Such a statement may apply to men like Schiller and John Sterling but it can hardly be said of one who lived to be sixty-four years old. If he had not been a remarkably patient, prudent, temperate and altogether practical man his disorder would have consumed him long before that time. It gave him no margin for wilfulness. Except when he spoke in public, his life was regulated with mathematical accuracy. There was something almost death-like in his self-control, and yet at times that also had to give way. If he had lived otherwise his case would have grown continually worse. The only recreation he had was working in his garden, and an occasional game of billiards. Four or five times a year he would go to a symphony concert, to hear Matthew Arnold lecture, or to see a distinguished actor. People who blamed him for not recovering his health knew not what they did. A Philadelphia doctor has made himself quite famous by curing women who have become nervous and debilitated from an unhealthy mode of life and drinking strong tea, but that is a very different thing from curing a true nervous disorder. Sumner's case was almost exceptional. He was cured in three years by Dr. Brown-Sequard and made perfectly well; but he had temperament, climate, and everything that money might give, in his favor. A good many invalids have been helped by Brown-Sequard after other doctors had failed to help them. A sturdy New Hampshire farmer wounded his foot with an axe and was supposed to have split a nerve in it. The wound healed perfectly but he never was able to do a whole day's work afterward. An oarsman in the international regatta of 1869 who was a man of enormous physical strength, deranged his nerves in some way and shot himself rather than endure the kind of life that was forced upon him.

The Wasson family was of Ulster-Irish descent, or as it is often improperly called Scotch-Irish. There is little Scotch blood in Ulster however, and the Wassons claimed to be descended from the Lollard heretics who were driven out of England in Henry the Fifth's time. John C. Calhoun belonged also to this class of men, who are noted for their industry, sobriety, mental vigor and inflexible tenacity. The county of Ulster contains only about one-eighth of the population of Ireland and yet it pays forty-six per cent of the Irish taxes. David Wasson, Senior, was trial justice for Brooksville, and was greatly dreaded by disorderly persons. He presided with dignity, and maintained better order than is often found in a country court-room. Wasson himself was more than Saxon; he was a German in mind, body and character, though he never went to Germany till after he was fifty. He had a German figure, much like his father's but broader; high square shoulders, a straight forehead and wide mouth. His features were strong and refined without being specially handsome. His brow was very fine and the eyes beneath it of so clear a blue as to be noticeable even at some distance.

There are men whom it is a delight to be with, whose "actions are as pleasant as roses," whose absence we regret as soon as they leave the room; but Wasson was not one of these. He had no personal charm like Longfellow or Wendell Phillips. He was more of a gentleman than many who pride themselves on that distinction, and he had very good manners, but not a very good style. A noted snob of those days and parasite of distinguished people said that he could have no faith in the genius of a man who dressed like Mr. Wasson. He would probably have dressed much better if he had possessed more abundant means, but I never saw him dressed in a way that anyone could rightfully complain of. His voice was pleasant but there was neither grace nor elegance in his speech. Usually it was direct, forcible, monotonous, with a very distinct enunciation; but sometimes it became drawling and wearisome with a peculiar accent on certain words which struck the ear too pointedly. This however was only among his friends; it did not happen in public. But all thought of human imperfections vanished as soon as he began to talk on one of his favorite topics; and there was a long list of them. You recognized that you were in the presence of a master mind, an analytical genius, who could take the world to pieces and put it together before your very eyes.

His conversation was better than his writing; in form, in freedom, and in warmth of feeling. He must have been the finest talker of his time. Carlyle could match him perhaps in quite a different manner; but I have never heard of any others. Lowell was what would have been called in Shakespeare's time a "witty and conceited gentleman" and John Weiss still more so; but neither of them could give the flow of original thought which came from Wasson like a pure mountain stream. Neither were they such complete masters of their subject. Like Carlyle he required suitable auditors to bring him forth at his best: but while Carlyle was mightiest when, his hearers were opposed to him Wasson always needed a somewhat sympathetic audience. If he saw unfriendly faces around him his ideas became congealed and his discourse controversial. At other times it was like following the course of a great unknown river, full of grand views and surprising discoveries. Nothing interests like imagination, or is more wholesome than good criticism. Yet he had no desire to be an autocrat of the drawing-room. He welcomed the opinions of others and encouraged free discussion. No man could be more ready to accept amendments to his propositions. Pride of opinion was nowhere to be found in him: he was only too modest and unassuming. If his friends did not agree with him he would reply with a mildly interrogative "Yes?" and then proceed as before. The finest rhetoric and even splendid oratory seemed poor compared with the plain statement of this unswerving seeker of the truth.

His knowledge was prodigious. He was a good linguist, a fine mathematician and versed in all the different schools of philosophy. He knew English literature as well as Macaulay; French and German as well as Carlyle. There seemed to be no period of history with which he was unacquainted. He remembered everything. If he had not read a book he had heard of it and had a pretty clear notion of what it contained. The only picture-gallery he ever visited was the small National Gallery in London, but from the few master-pieces he saw there he formed a quite correct judgment of the art of painting and could talk about any picture in an interesting way. He had also a good ear for music and divided with Lowell the honor among American literati of being able to appreciate music of the best quality. Besides this, his knowledge of practical affairs such as farming, gardening, housebuilding, fishing, sailing and other industrial arts was well-nigh endless also. How his head, which was not one of the largest, could contain it all I do not know. He could not recite the odes of Horace from memory; but he was able to repeat lengthy quotations from both English and foreign authors, and that without ever having committed them. In religious writings and controversies he was as much at home as a good lawyer in the statutes. In his wanderings he had become acquainted with many curious, strange and original people, and had gained their confidence by his friendly, open-hearted manner. Perhaps he had learned as much from the great book of human nature as from all other books; so that his fund of information was fairly inexhaustible. He may almost be said to have contained the material for another Shakespeare.

In 1877 just after the Turco-Russian war had begun we found him one evening in a smoking-car on the railway, surrounded by a crowd of young men who were listening eagerly to his account of the various wars which had already taken place between Russia and Turkey, and the political significance of the present one. "A man who possesses such a fund within has need of little from without." He cannot be called poor so long as he has a roof to shelter him and a single suit of clothes. Yet the acquisition of knowledge was never with Wasson for its own sake, though a good deal of adventitious knowledge came to him incidentally, but always for the attainment of wisdom. He did not believe in the Emersonian doctrine of obtaining inspiration through nature. "That was not the way," he would say, "in which the great minds of history became what they were. If we are to do lasting work we must know what the world is made of. Emerson himself does not work in that way." He quoted Schiller as saying, "He who would do benefit to the age in which he lives must bathe deep in the spirit of classical antiquity and then return to his own time to be in it, but not of it." That is, if we are to move the world with Archimedes' lever, we must have an historical basis to rest on. If a man ever had this it was Wasson. He went back to the Vedas in his study of religion; to the German forests and the pyramids in his investigation of politics and history. It was this which gave his arguments such cogency and made his discourse so fresh, vigorous and original. Arguments, however, will only serve for reasonable people. The ram that butted the locomotive had to learn from experience.

His sincerity was absolute. A devoted friend says of him: "During twelve years of familiar intercourse and eight more of less frequent communication, I never knew him once to take on the slightest color of insincerity. For it is not only in the use of words but in the tone of voice, the expression of the face and the movement of the body that duplicity can be detected." Like Sumner, he would rather lose a case than make use of an unfair argument. This may seem to many a super-sensitive morality, but it was not so for the work which these men had to do. Wasson believed in telling lies; to save life, to protect innocence, or even to prevent people from obtaining information which they had no right to. He considered it justifiable not only to deceive insane people, but also those demented creatures who do more mischief than lunatics because they cannot be shut up.

The more honor to him therefore for his truthfulness. In the case of a strong temperance woman who refused to allow a gentleman to marry her daughter unless he took the pledge, which he did with the deliberate intention of breaking it afterwards, he said, "I do not like to approve of his action, but she might just as well have held a pistol to his head." Neither did his own virtue make him uncharitable towards others. He recognized how impossible it is for servants and many other people to be always veracious, and claimed that the impostures practised by Frederick in the Seven Years' War might be justified by the strait he was in and the importance of the matter in hand. The main thing was to do honest work. For careless, sleazy, or fraudulent work he had no patience. He was greatly amused at the story of Dr. Francia ordering an army contractor who had cheated the government of Paraguay to be promenaded for an hour under the gallows, and he wished that more of them might be treated in that manner. He thought the torrent of mendacity which accompanies our presidential elections must have a bad influence on the morals of the American people.

The question of veracity was once discussed at the Chestnut Street Club, and Emerson said that Desdemona's lie seemed to him the best thing in the play of Othello. But there is, as Plato remarks, a more insidious evil than the deception of others and that is deceiving oneself. To detect an intentional falsehood is not very difficult, but when people tell lies with perfect assurance of their own sincerity the confusion that results is endless. The wisest of men are some times misled in this way. When we try to deceive others we have before us the danger of public exposure, while in self-deception we have only our own consciences to deal with. Neither do the two always go hand in hand. There are persons who are formally careful in regard to the truth, and yet live in perpetual delusion. Wasson recognized this danger and protected himself against it by a constant and severe self-examination. He knew himself at least better than most, and if he erred anywhere it was in too moderate an opinion of his own value. He had visually a clear consciousness of what he was about, in spite of his lively imagination.

He was in fact an American Doctor Johnson: a large hearted, high minded, sympathetic and logical *man*; and it is only a pity that he had not some Boswell of a friend who could have recorded his wise sayings and valuable criticism of men and things. He was more of an idealist than Doctor Johnson, and at the same time like Doctor Johnson in personal solidity, his English aplomb of character. They were both men of sterling quality. He was in all things especially human. His sympathies equalled the breadth of his mind. There was scarcely a subject in which he did not take an interest, and was not ready to converse on. As soon as he obtained a little money he wanted to help those who were in lack of it. His sister's husband being out of work, he designed the model for a small yacht and gave him an order for it. He had known the depths of human misery, and could make his experience of benefit to his friends. Poignant grief for the loss of a relative I think he never knew, and yet he did not neglect his duty to those in affliction, little as such duty might be expected of him. He was not a humorist or wit, and his conversation was only saved from dryness by its elevated tone; but he had a quick appreciation of the wit of others, and would sometimes laugh as heartily as Carlyle's professor in "Sartor Resartus." Ridicule and those books which are written to make people laugh were intolerable to him. He had a large stock of anecdotes at command, but he used them wisely and sparingly. He was refined as only a poet can be.

The general public, as Balzac says, judges only by results; and those who were themselves only practical in some specialty, or had made fortunes for themselves out of the gratuity of nature, were wont to look upon Wasson as a visionary and unpractical person. To those who acted only from motives of self-interest he was a perpetual puzzle. Neither was he ignorant of this unfavorable opinion, for he could see through people almost as if they were glass, and he endured it with true Emersonian serenity. If they had known what he thought of them they would not have felt so very comfortable. He was sufficiently practical for the profession to which he belonged, though not so diplomatic as some of them are. He could be diplomatic enough on occasion, and knew how to preserve an impenetrable secrecy when necessity required. He was too sensitive, and too dead-in-earnest to make much of an orator, but he was an effective speaker, and if he had remained in the law he would no doubt have made a success of it, and very likely would have become a member of Congress.

His adventure with a drunken sea-captain, while crossing from England in a sailing vessel has become proverbial. He probably saved the ship, and the lives of all on board, for a terrific storm arose immediately afterwards, the worst he had ever known, such as only a sober captain could possibly have weathered. There never was a better seaman when he was himself, so Wasson said. His judgment in regard to the investment of money, buying or selling a house, or in most of the small affairs of life, was excellent, and his advice in more serious matters so good that wise men might well have gone far to obtain it. Wherever he lived his house soon became conspicuous among all others for its refined air and tasteful appearance. In his half acre of a garden, he raised as fine fruit and vegetables as the most accomplished horticulturist, and even made wine from his own grapes equal to the best Californian. No man ever accomplished more with inadequate means. The interior of his house at West Medford had a pleasant style peculiarly its own. It reminded one of an old Dutch painting. In one of the last summers of his life he hybridized a seedling grape of large size and excellent flavor. He hoped to make a valuable property of this but his strength failed him too rapidly.

The house in West Medford was the only one he ever owned, and he gave a number of good reasons for purchasing it. It was cheap, and large enough for three people; there was a small garden with two fine apple-trees attached to it, and the salt water came almost to the foot of the garden. He had noticed also that the streets became dry after a rain more quickly in that portion of the town than elsewhere and judged from that it must be a healthy locality. He very quickly remodelled the place giving it the stamp of his own style and character.

He showed good judgment also in the education of his son George, now a marine-painter of well recognized merit. The boy inherited his father's sincerity and artistic feeling but not his intellectual tastes. In many respects he was more like his mother. He did not take to his studies nor was he fond of games, but liked bathing and sailing. When he was thirteen his father remarked that he did not know what he should be able to do with him. Well-intending friends said, you should get him a place in a store so that he may be earning something to help his parents, but Wasson replied: "No! I care too much for my boy to make a drudge of him for life, if it is possible for him to do better."

Soon after this George began to draw ships and naval engagements on the black-boards at school, and one of these was so good that the teacher gave an order to have it remain until his father could be called in to look at it. Wasson took notice of this talent in the boy and encouraged it, watching its development as time went on. There were no schools of art in Boston then, and one reason for his going to Germany in 1872 was to obtain systematic instruction for him in drawing and painting. Wasson's friends were now greatly discouraged. "What hope is there for him," they said, "in such a profession? It is not likely the boy is a genius, and who is going to purchase his pictures?" Yet his father persevered bravely in spite of many "outs" and temporary failures and finally lived to see the merit of his son admitted by those who were at first most sceptical of it. The son is now a fairly successful artist; especially noted for his skill in representing the motion of water and the attitude of floating vessels.

He was never prone to think evil, but he considered it a mischievous habit to try to think better of people than they were—an injustice to character and virtue. "Treat people better than they deserve," he would say, "but see them as they are." His kindness of heart now and then led him into difficulties which those who care more for their reputation than anything else, would have avoided. During his Arctic expedition Bradford took a number of stereopticon-views from icebergs and other indigenous scenery with the intention of exhibiting them in public on his return. This he finally did, more as a private celebration than with a hope of making money from it, and requested Wasson to assist him by giving an oral explanation of the pictures. Wasson wanted to say, "That is not my business," but he felt under great obligation to Mr. Bradford for the partial recovery of his strength, and did not like to refuse. He had no conception however of what was in store for him. He sent to Bradford for a list of the different views and prepared an address suitable for the occasion; but when the performance took place Bradford either forgot this or lost his presence of mind, for he exhibited the pictures without order or regularity, so that Wasson soon became confused and was able to give but a very poor account of them. This affair was the more vexatious because it was quite impossible to give any explanation of it.

Matthew Arnold distinguishes between Plato as a great writer and thinker and Aristotle, who is only a great thinker. In this respect Wasson was more like Aristotle, though he resembled Plato again in being always an idealist. His writing shows the influence of his early studies in the law, and derives much of its virtue as well as some peculiarities from that source. It usually takes the form of an argument and is clear, logical and accurate, but also in style rather hard and dry. What it lacks is the pictorial element—what Carlyle possessed in such luxuriance. No law book ever was or could be written for entertainment, and those who expect to be amused by reading Wasson or Aristotle had better look elsewhere. His essays are like hard wood. He worked hard in writing them and we must work also when we read them. Sometimes we meet with passages in them of the purest, most limpid English, though these are more common in his later than his earlier writings. He said once, "I make no effort to please my readers, or even to obtain a graceful diction, I only try to say what I have to in the plainest manner." There is a decided charm in this perfect plainness, this absence of all decoration. One likes to think how old Vanderbilt had the brass and ornaments taken off the locomotives on the New York Central road. Telling the truth was Wasson's business in life, and he turned neither to the right nor the left in doing it.

However, he did not reach this philosophy at once. His earlier work is marred slightly by a love of the grotesque, a sort of plough-boy rhetoric, which is ill-assorted with the elevated character of his ideas. He suffers also occasionally by an hair-splitting attempt to prove his point beyond the possibility of contradiction. In two or three of his essays there is an unsuccessful effort for liveliness, the result of complaints from his magazine editors, and now and then will appear an unconscious imitation of Carlyle; but what does it all amount to? We are inundated now-a-days with writing that is perfect, or nearly so, in form and yet brings no message to mankind. It pleases the understanding, but it does not satisfy the soul. It gives us no new ideas: in fact ideas are hateful to it.

"Time and space conquering steam,
And the light-out-speeding telegraph
Bears nothing on its beam."

Wasson's writing compared with this is as an old-time stage-coach journey in which an interesting conversation, moral or political, is carried on by men like Fisher Ames and Rev. David Osgood, compared with the empty elegance and despatch of a modern railway-train. It is fresh because it is genuine; vigorous because it is manly; and original because it is true. He is more original than Carlyle, and so profound that it seems as if only a pearl-diver could follow him to such a depth. Yet his natural element is so pure, calm and tranquil, that we easily accomplish what seems at first an impossible descent. In "Epic Philosophy" he has dealt with the problem of good and evil in a manner more noble and penetrating than was ever before attempted. In his essay on the "Genius of Woman" he enters on a new and important field of investigation, a virgin soil as yet untried. In "Unity," the greatest of his essays, he boldly climbs the Jacob's ladder of philosophy and walks serene among the stars, grappling even with Infinity. He had achieved unity for himself; the one complete cosmopolitan mind of his time. In his highest flights he is never cold or inexorable, but always human, tender, and sympathetic. He loved the unkind, heedless world; life was wonderful to him. "What do I think of Wasson?" said Professor James of Harvard, a few days after his death, "I look upon him as one of the great instructors of mankind."

It was complained by a critic of Emerson's "Parnassus" that only two of Wasson's poems were to be found in that collection; and Alcott, who had a keen scent for superior literature, once turned a visitor out of his study for denying the superiority of Wasson's poetry. Many of his sonnets are gems, unsurpassed in any language, and the one called "Pride" seems to me in its grand simplicity to be without a rival. If there is any American poem which sings itself like "All's well," it is Longfellow's ballad of "Mary Garvin." "The Plover" has a pensive grace which is as rare as its subtile and elevated thought. They are however few in number and he did not think there was enough of them to publish in a volume. They were finally published *post mortem* in what was, if the truth be told, a rather unfortunate manner. Two of his finest sonnets, on "Silence" and "Wendell Phillips," were by mischance omitted, and a good many included that were either failures or written for some trifling occasion, and never intended for publication. As if to prevent all chance of popularity, the best pieces were placed at the close of the book and a long unfinished Hegelian poem at the beginning. Even the paper they were printed on was such as Wasson especially disliked. It seems a pity that he should have been denied this little celebrity.

He received better justice from Mr. Frothingham, who has published an excellent memoir of his life and work together with a number of his essays,—a handsome volume well bound and printed. Yet one cannot help thinking that here also the author's fame, as well as the interest of the general public, might have been better consulted by a more careful selection and a wider range of subjects. "Epic Philosophy" at least ought by no means to have been omitted, nor is there any example given of Wasson's fine literary criticism, in itself enough to have made a writer celebrated. His essay on Whittier is not only a just estimate, but seems also in its wise and tender application to include Whittier poetically, as the sea encircles an island. In this department of writing he was the equal of Lessing and almost of Goethe; but with characteristic modesty he celebrated Lowell as the first of American critics. Wasson's book notices in the "Boston Commonwealth" were most interesting reading and contained much of his finest thought.

His famous Groveland address was not directed against a faith in the divinity of Christ, for he held that belief in profound respect, as signifying the divine origin and mission of mankind. He considered every spiritually gifted person to be the result of an immaculate conception. At the close of the essay on "Unity" he says:

"Verily, I believe that he who was born at Bethlehem, that majestic witness for the soul, was Messias, Christ, one sent from the Father; that the eternal Godhood concurred in the production of his being; that the consciousness of a divine inhabitation lived in his heart."

It was no new evil he complained of, but one older than the brazen serpent in the wilderness. It might be called the fossilization of religious ideas. He called to his support the testimony of a witness whose orthodoxy has never been questioned. This was the poet Milton, who says:

"A man may be a heretic in the truth; and if he believe things only because his pastor says so, or the assembly so determine, without other reason, though his belief be true, yet the very truth he holds becomes his heresy."

Then Wasson adds: "And it is no more than a different application of this aphorism to say that one may be an idolater in the reverence of that which is truly venerable; for if he render it homage only in blind conformity to custom, and in implicit submission to the discipline of ancient use and wont, though the object be worthy, yet his worship is an idolatry." It is indeed a type of idolatry which becomes continually more subtle and dangerous with the progress of civilization.

In politics Wasson was a republican without being a democrat. He hailed the advent of the republican party in 1856 as indicating an improvement in our political consciousness. Democracy, he said, led to political selfishness and disintegration. He pointed out many years before Von Holst that the secession of the southern states was the legitimate fruit of democratic principles. He thought that suffrage ought not to be a right, but a privilege, the privilege of good citizenship. He was also the first to argue in favor of civil-service reform, and a selection of officials by competitive examination. He might have found sufficient arguments from experience, but he was not content with that. He went back to the first principles of political science as indicated in the social organization of mankind. He laid down the rule that society is not more for the benefit of the individual than the individual for the benefit of society; and our last war sufficiently proved the truth of this. When he first brought forward these arguments at the Boston Radical Club in 1879 he was met by a storm of opposition and almost personal invective. One reason for this was that a large portion of his audience was composed of what is sometimes called strong-minded women, who fully expected to acquire the right of suffrage on democratic principles. His hearers had been accustomed to think of a republic and a democracy as one and the same thing, and they could not understand Wasson at all. They concluded that he must be a monarchist, an emissary of Bismarck. They had no arguments to oppose him with, for it was a subject they had never reflected upon; so they complained that he was illiberal, re-actionary, and lacked faith in human nature. Since they were in a numerical majority they thought they had the best of the discussion, but the most impartial of his listeners did not find it so. Louisa Alcott said once after a lively discussion, in her decisive manner, "I like Mr. Wasson, and I admire the way in which he fights against odds." His views on politics were similar to those held by Washington, Adams, Hamilton, and most of the founders of the Constitution, as also by all the great minds of history, by Aristotle, Cicero, Dante, Shakespeare, Milton, and Leibnitz. Wasson however did not look to the past, but wished to improve in a rational manner on what we already have. He considered woman suffrage as a political monstrosity, and considered it even more dangerous in its tendencies than socialism.

The true reward of a man of genius lies not in his fame but in his influence. His celebrity is of more value to those who receive the rich gifts of his intellect than to himself. Wasson's direct influence during his life was limited to a very small circle; but who can tell how far it extended indirectly beyond this? To those who knew him the thought of this patient, indomitable truth-seeking hero was like an elixir of moral and spiritual vitality. So the orders of a field-marshal are carried to the generals of division, and from these pass onward till every private-soldier feels the impulse of a single will. Perhaps the time will come when he will be better appreciated. The future historian of our literature cannot well neglect so independent and original a thinker, and perhaps Americans of the next century may find him more congenial to their modes of thought than do those of the present era. If he lives at all, it is likely he will outlive every other writer of his time. One may read Plato or Bacon or Goethe, and then return to Wasson and still find something new and instructive in his essays—something we did not know before.

WENDELL PHILLIPS

If Hawthorne was the antipodes of Emerson, Wendell Phillips was of Wasson. One might form a proportion out of these four, in which Phillips and Hawthorne would be the extremes, and Emerson and Wasson the mean terms. He was, in his way, as perfect an artist as Hawthorne, while he differed from him as the sea does from the land. He was more like Emerson in his mental methods, and was a man of action. While he took the same interest in public affairs as Wasson, the slavery question was the only point on which the two could ever agree. One was an ardent and unreflecting revolutionist; the other a systematic thinker and conservative supporter of the general order of affairs.

When in 1870 he was candidate for governor of Massachusetts, on a hopeless ticket, and was taunted with being ambitious, he proudly replied, "Born of six generations of Yankees, I knew the way to office and turned my back on it thirty years ago." His family was one of the earliest and most generally respected in New England; and at one time was influential and flourishing, but now nearly extinct. Rev. George Phillips of Rainham in Norfolk, England, was a graduate of Cambridge University, and entered the Church of England, but soon became a dissenter, and embarked with Governor Winthrop on the ship Arabella, in 1630, for the western world. He was the first minister at Watertown; a position in those days as important as the presidency of a trunk line is in our own. Cotton Mather and the early writers speak of him almost as the founder of the Congregational Church in New England; and he and his descendants were all cultivated gentlemen. Two of his great-grandsons founded the preparatory academies at Andover and Exeter, called by that name. John Phillips, the father of Wendell, graduated at Harvard in 1788. He was the president of the Massachusetts senate for one term, and the first mayor of Boston, distinctly so called. His wife was a Miss Sarah Walley of Brookline, and Wendell himself was their eighth child, born November 29th, 1811—a year memorable for the appearance of a comet with six tails.

During his boyhood, the family lived in a large mansion house in Old Cambridge, which has since been occupied by Professor Andrews Norton and his son. In a large and amiable household, with a mother for whom he always showed the deepest respect, his earlier years must have been happy much beyond the lot of ordinary mortals. He was fitted for college at the Boston Latin School, where he was distinguished both for scholarship, faultless behavior, and fine declamations. Charles Sumner was his companion there, as well as in college and at the law-school. They are both said to have given striking proof of their oratorical talent, though perhaps not more so than many others have before and since. He entered at Harvard in 1827, while Sumner was a sophomore, and Dr. Holmes and his celebrated twenty-niners were in their junior year. His college life was a dream of wonder-land. Rich, gifted, full of good-humor, handsome in form and feature, a brilliant scholar, he seemed above all others to be Fortune's favored child. Work was easy to him, and his play was the sport of genius. He was everywhere among the first; president of the Porcellian Club, president and orator of the Hasty Pudding Club—the Apollo Belvedere of his classmates. He also belonged to a society called "The Owls," which only met at midnight, and the one who could control his face so as to look most like an owl was considered the best fellow.

Yet in the midst of this happiness, like the Hindoo prince, the spirit of sadness comes over him when he reflects that very few are so fortunate as himself, and that a great many seem to be born to positive misfortune. The change in him was so marked that his classmates took notice of it and attributed it to too much of a religious interest; but it was not that. He accepted religion as he found it, and lived and died in the faith of his ancestors. What is called a religious experience never came to him; but from this time forward he showed an especial tenderness and consideration for unfortunate people. It is well we bear this trait of his character in mind, for it is the interpretation of the various phases of his career.

He studied law, but does not appear to have ever taken a serious interest in it. Sumner, on the contrary, became a shining light in the law-school, and there laid the solid foundation of his future eminence.

Looking back at the past, we see now how the lives of these two men diverged. In tact and readiness, in mental gifts, and fineness of nature, Phillips was slightly the superior of Sumner, but Sumner easily surpassed him in greatness of design. Phillips wished to be an orator, and afterwards confessed that at this period of his life his admiration for Webster knew no legitimate bounds. But oratory is an art which requires a liberal profession for its basis; and Webster and Sumner became orators by virtue of their profession. An orator merely as such is simply an actor, and it requires a strong and well-balanced character to withstand the temptations of the stage and the platform. Wendell Phillips afterwards found a basis for his oratory in the anti-slavery conflict; and then, when that came to an end, his occupation was gone. It is also to be doubted if he had the right sort of intellect to make a lawyer of, though no man could be better qualified in other respects for practice in the courts.

Although one of his professors predicted a term in Congress for him, he did not obtain any clients for several years; which is more remarkable as there could have been no question in regard to his capacity or popularity. Another strange fact is that when he went to Europe and asked Judge Story for letters-of-introduction, he failed to obtain them; while Sumner, who was Story's favorite, was presented a few days later with more than a dozen. Had Judge Story already discovered a centrifugal and uncontrollable element in the man?

It is difficult to understand, at this distance, the persecution of the early abolitionists. They were the most harmless and inoffensive of men, and the spirit in which they approached the slavery question, and the arguments they used in regard to it, were like those by which the Christian Church obtained the abolition of serfdom in Europe. They were the most purely Christian people of their time; certainly much better Christians than those ministers of the gospel who denounced them as disturbers of a hollow peace. So Suetonius speaks of the Christians as being disturbers of the peace, and Tacitus, like a late writer in the "Atlantic Monthly," refers to them as enemies of society.

It is true they finally became narrow-minded, intolerant, and almost misanthropic, as always happens when a small minority are fatally enclosed within an unfriendly community; but they were not so in the beginning. Their methods were mild and pacific: they wished to influence public-opinion, and even hoped to persuade the slaveholders to assist in general emancipation. That the slave-holder should have been somewhat irritated at this suggestion to part with so much valuable property is not surprising; but why should it have disturbed their neighbors in Massachusetts and Connecticut where the question of free and slave labor had been agitated forty years before, and satisfactorily settled? The same speakers who harangued against the abolitionists, would say in the next breath that it was contrary to democratic principles for people in one section of the country to concern themselves about the affairs of those in another. Was it an inherited public tendency from the spirit of intolerance which formerly persecuted the Quakers? However that may be, it is an historical fact that great social reformers always have begun in a similar manner, and their importance can fairly be measured by the violence and duration of the opposition to them.

Wendell Phillips did not at first take an interest in the anti-slavery cause. The abolitionists were not personally known to him, and his mind was largely occupied with the pleasures of fashionable society, where he shone before all others. There was a certain strength and good sense in this; the reserve of a man who waits for opportunity, and who does not risk shipwreck at the start by rushing hastily into troubled waters. In October 1837, he was married to Miss Mary Anna Green, the daughter of Benjamin Green of Boston, and cousin, or other near relative, to Mrs. Maria Chapman, a friend of Harriet Martineau and other English philanthropists. In November occurred the riot at Alton, Illinois, and the assassination of Lovejoy. Dr. Channing's first petition for an indignation-meeting in Faneuil Hall was refused by the authorities; but a second and more urgent one was granted: evidently with the anticipation that the anti-slavery people might, after all, find themselves in a minority.

As it happened, the audience was nearly divided between the two parties, but the pro-slavery faction, led by government officials, had the advantage of being able to make all the noise and disturbance they wished without being interfered with by the police for it. It seemed as if the meeting would end in confusion and a vote of disagreement. Twenty-five years later Wendell Phillips said of it: "I went there without the least intention of making a speech or taking any part in the proceedings. My wife and Mrs. Chapman wished to go, and I accompanied them. I remember wearing a long surtout, a brand-new one, with a small cape (as was the fashion of the day), and after the attorney-general made his speech denouncing Lovejoy as a fool, I suddenly felt myself inspired, and tearing off my overcoat, started for the platform. My wife seized me by the arm, half terrified, and said, 'Wendell, what are you going to do?' I replied, 'I am going to *speak*, if I can make myself heard.'" The uproar was so great that the chairman asked Dr. Channing if he could stand thunder; but the personal beauty and intrepidity of Phillips,—coming like a meteor out of the night,—so surprised all hearers, that they paused to listen to him, and were so charmed by his eloquence that they neglected to make any further disturbance. The attorney-general was wholly discomfited, and Dr. Channing's resolutions were carried by a substantial majority.

It is surprising that so thorough an historian as Von Holst should have omitted to make mention of this speech, which really struck the key-note of the anti-slavery movement from first to last. As we have it now, revised by its author from the newspaper reports of the time, it is one of the purest, most spontaneous and magnetic pieces of oratory in existence. It deserves a place beside those two famous speeches of James Otis and Patrick Henry which ushered in the war of separation from England. It possesses even a certain advantage, in the fact that it never has been nor is likely to be made use of for school declamations. It will always remain fresh, vigorous, and original as when it was first delivered.

But Phillips was not content merely with silencing the opposition. He claimed that the cause for which he spoke, and for which the meeting had been called, was one of higher importance than any that had preceded it in Faneuil Hall. When the audience murmured at this, he boldly continued: "Insomuch as *thought* is better than *money*, is the cause for which Lovejoy died superior to that for which our ancestors contended. James Otis thundered within these walls when the king did but touch his pocket; imagine his indignant eloquence if they had attempted to put a gag upon his lips." For this statement, if for nothing else, Wendell Phillips deserves an immortality in the history of his country.

With such an achievement at the age of twenty-six, what might not have been expected of his maturer years,—of the full fruition of his genius? What but a future candidate for the senate of the United States, or even for the presidency? The full fruition of his genius, the development that nature intended for him, never was realized. It is true, he accomplished much, and was in himself even more,—but by no means what he might have been. Even in the first hour of success, the temptation comes to us which determines our future destiny in one way or another.

The two ladies were of course delighted at his triumph, and overwhelmed him with congratulations; but Mrs. Chapman, "the born duchess", as she was called, saw instantly what an advantage would accrue to the small band of abolitionists from the alliance of this able young aristocrat, with his suddenly revealed gift. That evening she used all the arts of persuasion to induce him to relinquish his profession and cast his fortune to sink or swim on the broad ocean of reform. She argued that Webster and Everett had the field; that years must elapse before he could win equality with those veterans; while as an anti-slavery orator, a fresh field would be open to his genius, in which he would meet with no competitor. The hour only waited for the man, and what a glorious reward to have finally secured—the freedom of a whole race! Unhappily this coincided with a natural inclination in Phillips, of which we have already spoken, and a few days later he decided to follow her advice.

One could heartily wish that the born duchess had left Wendell Phillips to work out his own salvation. It is hardly the sign of a strong character for a man to be guided in the choice of a profession by feminine counsel; but he was still young, tender-hearted, and susceptible, and if left to himself might have escaped the impending danger. It was a temptation at once to his ambition as an orator and the latent heroism in him,—his disposition to self-sacrifice. His law practice was not satisfactory, and he could not look forward to immediate success in that direction—especially since the Faneuil Hall meeting.

Much better however for him to have gone patiently forward in the path already cleared by Webster and Everett, until, fully equipped in experience and maturity, he could have carried his anti-slavery principles into the arena of practical politics and become a leader in the House of Representatives, or have stood by Sumner in the Senate. A woman can hardly be expected to understand the long-drawn persistent struggle by which a man rises to the top of his profession; but it seems as if Mrs. Chapman might have been more considerate of the fortune and prospects of this young Apollo, himself of more value than many negroes. He did not properly belong with the abolitionists. They always felt so. They were excellent people, stainless in thought and in action, but limited in education and ability. Men of the highest mental endowments naturally form a class by themselves, though not an exclusive one. If Phillips had consulted John Quincy Adams on the subject, he would have been answered with a "No" such as might have been heard across Court Street.

His life was now as much changed as if spring had suddenly been succeeded by winter. It was like a penitential pilgrimage. He had inherited from his father a moderate property upon which he and his wife, who was already much of an invalid, could live in a moderate way. He resided for a time in Florence, Massachusetts, and then purchased a small house in Essex Street, Boston, which has since been torn down to make room for the extension of Harrison Avenue. It was a house of very small dimensions, such as is commonly occupied by a mechanic's family; but possessed the advantage of admitting as much sunshine as possible into Mrs. Phillips' lonely chamber, which was probably his reason for selecting it. He wished to live economically in order to save money for the cause of freedom, and also for private charities.

The number of persons whom he assisted in the course of his life may be called countless; and he was even too careful in preventing a knowledge of this from being made public. He selected for his motto the Latin sentence which he had translated while at school, "Phocian always remained poor, though he might have been very rich." His fashionable friends deserted from him in a body, and old family acquaintances passed him in the street without recognition. The only society he had was his wife and Mrs. Chapman and the families of the few abolitionists who lived in Boston. He was as careful of his diet, exercise, and sleep, as a trainer is in regard to a race-horse; and was rewarded for this with the most magnificent health. In all things he illustrated the words of the poet:—

> "The hero is not fed on sweets;
> Daily his own heart he eats:
> The chambers of the great are jails
> And head winds right for royal sails."

He never lost an opportunity of speaking on the slavery question. He joined the corps of lyceum-lecturers, and soon won the first place among them. If they would listen to him on slavery, or "Toussaint L'Ouverture," his lecture was free; otherwise it must be paid for. No one else did so much to arouse public consideration in regard to this great evil, as the conservative Webster had already designated it. All through the northern states, wherever the railroads went, there Wendell Phillips was also, exhorting the people with burning words, and warning especially the farmers and laboring classes that free and slave labor could not exist together, and unless the negroes were emancipated they would ultimately become enslaved themselves.

Stumping New England, it was said, made Wendell Phillips an orator; and that, after all, was the right name for it. It was refined and elegant as could be, but still stump-oratory. It became so inevitably from the nature of the case, and in one sense this is to his credit, for it would seem to prove that he cared more for the cause than for his own reputation. He never attained to the well-considered architectural oratory of Webster and Burke, though in his best period he sometimes came very close to this, but neither did he speak to the House of Commons, nor before a bench of judges. Nothing is more fatiguing to untrained minds than a consistent and elaborate argument; and the mixed character of Phillips' speeches, like a bonfire made out of all inflammable materials, was remarkably well suited to the audiences whom he addressed. It is said that even Burke often emptied the benches, as if his associates in parliament did not appreciate him so well as those who now enjoy reading his works.

An artist who draws with a free hand, will be able to develop his talent to its full extent, but one who draws in a cramped or false manner will always suffer more or less from the effects of it; but this was not the worst of the matter. Self-control does much for the artist, but unprejudiced criticism is also necessary. This Phillips never could obtain. There were persons who judged him impartially, but he was not in the way of obtaining their opinions. He was surrounded by a small band of adherents who praised him without discrimination, and who fiercely repelled the attacks of those who found fault with him. The newspapers all took sides against him, for both political parties dreaded the agitation of the slavery question, and Phillips could rarely look into one of them without meeting with a savage attack on himself by some subaltern who knew of no better use for his quill than the manufacture of these venomous darts. Neither could he walk through the streets of Boston without hearing himself cursed and execrated. Meanwhile Mrs. Chapman and Mrs. L. Maria Child extolled him to the skies. Faithful and undistorted picture of himself he could meet with nowhere.

We read of saintly characters who have endured persecution with Christian humility and resignation, who have blessed those who cursed them, and loved those who hated them; but how many such have we been personally acquainted with? If we except Desdemona there are none in the great dramatists. It is an excellent principle, this of returning good for evil; but is it not also true that nature has planted hatred in us as a protection against future imposition? There may be such personages, but Wendell Phillips was not one of them.

He endured the stings of the pro-slavery hornets, as they were called, with stoical dignity and forbearance, but in spite of all good resolutions, they had an effect upon the inner man. Like the good Maritornes when Sancho Panza mistook her for an evil spirit, he endured the drubbing as long as flesh-and-blood would stand it, and then retaliated in good earnest. It was discovered at length, that Wendell Phillips had a sharp tongue, as well as a silver one, and could use it also with some temper. Of course he was blamed for this, and very few considered what provocation he had, or gave him credit for his previous forbearance. The habit increased rather than abated in him with age, and finally acquired the nature of a familiar demon that would appear unexpectedly in the midst of a brilliant discourse and sadly mar the effect of it.

His tendency to exaggeration, disregard of fact, and recklessness of statement, may all be attributed to his irregular, improvised manner of working. There are few public speakers, indeed, who escape these faults. What preparation he made for his speeches will probably never be known. He was always as mysterious on this point as a professional juggler. To a lady who once asked him about it, he replied, that he never made any preparation. For those of his speeches that have been published, we are obliged to a skilful short-hand writer named Yerrinton, who was Wendell Phillips' devoted admirer, and never missed an opportunity of hearing him on a fresh subject in Boston or New York.

To judge from internal evidence, it would seem likely that having divided his subject, as a lawyer does his argument, into a number of points, and having filled his mind somewhat full of them, he wrote out a careful and well-studied opening to his address, and then committed it to memory. This would enable him to make terms, as it were, with his audience in those first critical moments of his speech, and afterwards he could rely on his native wit and genius to carry him through. When his subject was a criticism of public events, this was not so difficult, and it gave him the advantage of a certain vivacious energy which appealed strongly to his hearers; but it was a dangerous practice. An orator who has a certain length of time to fill, and a reputation to sustain, is obliged to go on at all hazards. He cannot afford to be dull, nor to stop for a moment's reflection. If his memory fails him for an instant, imagination must supply its place. In this manner he often made misstatements which were quite unintentional, and must have been deeply regretted afterwards. Some allowance too should be made for a man who feels himself in a desperate position. His historical lectures on "The Lost Arts," "Daniel O'Connel," and "Toussaint," must sooner or later have been committed to memory, and were repeated again and again in a nearly identical form.

To amend for these deficiencies, his delivery was perfect, and even more than that. One of our best critics has called him matchless in this respect, and no other orator of the century, except possibly Canning, may be compared to him. Webster was more effective, but rather ponderous. Choate's style was peculiar, and Everett's cold and studied. Gladstone resembles him more, perhaps, than any other, but Gladstone has a decided solemnity of manner which is a help to him among his countrymen, but a defect as judged by classic standards. With Wendell Phillips, it was not only that every phase of thought and feeling was portrayed at once in his face, attitude, and gestures, but this was done with such grace and purity as only belongs to the very highest art. It was as if a figure in Raphael's "School at Athens" had suddenly stepped out from the picture and explained the thought of the master to us in words.

There is nothing I can compare with the unconscious grace and purity of Phillips in his best moments except a picture by Raphael, or one of Milton's shorter poems. It was no lurid brilliancy or artificial light that shone from him, but rather the cheerful radiance of spring sunshine. No matter how gloomy the political outlook might be, or in what sombre colors he depicted it, this light from the man himself illuminated his subject and gave encouragement to his hearers. The most prolonged applause could not disturb a muscle in his countenance, and a storm of hisses appeared to have as little effect on him. From the first word to the last, he was master of the platform, and no one dreamed of contesting his right to it. His gestures were his own, and could not be imitated, for they were the creation of the moment. There was something magical in this art of his, and if his wisdom and judgment had only equalled it, he might have counted among the greatest of men.

Emerson sent one of Webster's orations to Carlyle, and the latter complained that it was monotonous and lacked the poetic quality of Demosthenes. This is quite true, but at the same time it may be said that Webster's speeches, judged simply as literature, have not been surpassed by five other American writers. The grand roll of his sentences does not become wearisome to a lover of sound reasoning, and in the presentation of his subject he has rarely been equalled. An oration of his is not like a picture hanging on the wall, but rather a public building which one can walk around and look at from the four cardinal points. Even his speech on the fugitive-slave bill, for which he has been so much blamed, contains the best analysis of the slavery question up to that time which had yet been made. He considered slavery a great evil, and his mistake evidently consisted in supposing that a great evil could exist in one part of the nation without vitiating the whole of it.

Phillips looked upon slavery as a crime, and attacked it in an uncompromising manner. His speeches are not much like Webster's, but they are excellent reading; full of keen, vivid thought, bright sayings, and genial humor. He had the imagination of Demosthenes, but without the logical faculty. Many of them possess historical value, and but for too much *voix blanc*, like the brightness of new silver, might be compared with Emerson's essays. Certain passages and individual sentences are of rare beauty. Speaking of Lovejoy thirty years after his death, he said, "How cautiously men sink into nameless graves, while now and then one forgets himself into immortality." At the time of the Dred Scott decision, he exclaimed: "Is Liberty dead? Is the valley of the Mississippi her grave? Are the Rocky Mountains her monument; and shall the Falls of Niagara chant forever her requiem?" In his Brooklyn address of November 1st, 1859, the finest of his orations, and one which he must have prepared with exceptional care, after telling the story of Tsar Nicholas, who insisted on building a straight railroad from Moscow to St. Petersburg in spite of the opposition of the engineers, he continued: "An intelligent democracy says of slavery, or a law, or a creed, 'This is justice, or it is not'; the track of God's thunderbolt is a straight line from justice to iniquity, and the church or state that cannot stand it must get out of the way." Or take this illustration of his subject from Athenian life — which is itself Athenian, and very much in the vein of Demosthenes: —

"Anacharsis went into the forum at Athens, and heard a case argued by the great minds of the day, and saw the vote. He walked out into the streets, and somebody said to him, 'What think you of Athenian liberty?' 'I think,' said he, 'wise men argue causes, and fools decide them.' Just what the timid scholar two thousand years ago said in the streets of Athens, that which calls itself the scholarship of the United States says today of popular agitation, that it lets wise men argue questions, and fools decide them. But that unruly Athens, where fools decided the gravest questions of polity and right and wrong, where it was not safe to be just, and where property, which you had garnered up by the thrift and industry of to-day, might be wrung from you by the caprices of the mob to-morrow,—that very Athens probably secured the greatest human happiness and nobleness of its era, invented art, and sounded for us the depths of philosophy: God lent to it the noblest intellects, and it flashes to-day the torch that gilds yet the mountain-peaks of civilization."

At a memorial meeting of Sumner's friends in 1874, Phillips concluded his remarks with the same expression that Cicero used in regard to Homer:— "There was no one like Sumner." He was not a mellow-toned orator of peace and conciliation, but soul-stirring, and one could detect the distant flash of a sword-blade in his periods.

In private life, he was the most delightful of men. Good orators always have the finest manners, for it is from them that we learn the art of behavior; but Wendell Phillips never brought the great man of the world to the drawing-room or dining-table, but was so perfectly a gentleman that he seemed almost like a prince who had abdicated his hereditary possessions. He did not seem to have been bred to good manners, but born to them, so natural and unconstrained was everything he said and did. Never self-conscious and never self-forgetful; where consideration was needed he was sure to be at hand. He was at once dignified and deferential, even to children and servants, whom he was sure to remember in the homes where he visited, and usually had a kind word for them at the right moment. I do not think he could have treated even the meanest of women with disrespect.

He never talked too long or too brilliantly, but seemed to be on the watch to give everyone present a fair chance. His presence in a room was stimulating, and made people brighter than their ordinary wont. Of small conversation, conversational pleasantries, and what is called table-talk, he happily knew nothing. He had no sharp wit or repartee, but plenty of genial humor, and could of course tell a story to perfection. His imitations of other orators were highly amusing, especially what he called Webster's Rochester speech: "The public debt; it must be paid; and it *shall* be paid;—how much is it?" He would go through the performance and then resume his seat at the table, laughing like a child. When Emerson and Phillips dined together they would look at one another, as it seemed, with a kind of awe, as if they were more wonderful to each other than to ordinary mortals. It was after such an occasion that Emerson said, "This man is such a perfect artist that he ought to be walking all the galleries of Europe, and yet here he is fighting these hard questions." He did not appear to care much for society however, and always declined an invitation where he was in danger of being lionized, or otherwise made use of.

A characteristic anecdote is told of him during the expedition of the abolitionists to England in 1853. They were entertained there by their British allies, and also by members of the nobility. A certain duchess (or countess perhaps) invited them to a lawn-party, and while they were engaged in drinking coffee on her lawn, an uncomfortable drizzling mist came down on the company. The gentlemen all carried their hats in their hands, out of respect for the duchess, who wore a sort of lace tiara; but in this emergency Phillips, who had a speech to make at Birmingham next evening, placed his on his head and continued to wear it. The consequence was that when the duchess gave them a second entertainment Phillips was not invited. He was as independent as this on all occasions.

The anti-slavery movement carried along with it a variety of other social and political movements such as spiritualism, total abstinence, and the prevention of capital punishment; which prevented many sympathetic friends of the cause from joining it, and gave it a quaint, and sometimes even a comical aspect. These Utopian and impracticable notions were accepted by the abolitionists partly on the log-rolling principle, and partly from a tendency of those people to separate themselves from what is real and tangible. It seems strange that a man of Wendell Phillips' culture and mental endowments should not have been able to distinguish between a necessary and possible reform, and those vague theories of human happiness and perfection which are not based on the logic of experience, but indicate rather a wayward mental condition in the devotees. If a little knowledge is a dangerous thing, what should be said of unripe and superficial thinking? We wonder what were Wendell Phillips' reflections concerning the women in Bloomer costume, and the paradoxical persons who frequented the anti-slavery fairs, and created disturbances at the anti-slavery conventions. If questioned about them he would probably have said, with a laugh, "Oh, those are our barnacles;" but they were only extreme cases of the general tendency.

It was not the right element for a man of his calibre: he did not become a spiritualist, nor was he so intolerant as to object to the use of brandy for cooking purposes; but he published an injudicious and even intemperate letter to the chief-justice of Massachusetts and the president of Harvard College, arraigning them for drinking wine at a public banquet. He exerted himself strenuously to obtain the repeal of capital punishment; and when that failed, and also an attempt to obtain a pardon for a miserable murderer, whom it was merely a kindness to hang, he attacked the governor of the state in a sermon before the Theodore Parker Society, which was little better than a tirade of invectives. He never appeared as an advocate of woman suffrage before the public, but he is said to have approved of it. Neither would he go to the polls to vote; at first because the national constitution supported slavery, and afterwards because the government maintained an army and encouraged war.

He missed a fine opportunity to escape from this narrow routine and enter the arena of practical politics when the Free-soil party was formed to prevent the extension of slavery. However, he either did not think of it, or preferred to hold fast to his former friends, though he little knew how little they cared for him, and he continued for ten years longer to lecture on Toussaint and talk moral-suasion,—riding hard on the Garrisonian formula. It seems like small business when we recollect the work that Seward and Sumner and Chase were doing meanwhile.

It was the attack on Harper's Ferry that broke the spell at last, and awoke Wendell Phillips to a higher and more useful life. It is difficult to realize now, the courage that was required to appear before the public in defence of what was generally considered the outrage of a madman. It is easier for men to understand the differential calculus, than that rebellion against government is either the greatest of crimes or the highest of virtues. When government becomes so bad that honesty and virtue cannot endure it, revolution is imminent. Phillips, Emerson and Thoreau, John A. Andrew and Rev. J. M. Manning, pastor of the Old South church, were the ones who asserted this. Andrew and his friends called a meeting, nominally to obtain funds for the wife and daughters of John Brown. The hall was crowded with a remarkably intelligent looking class of people. Andrew presided, and claimed that whatever might be thought of his Virginia raid, John Brown himself, considered from his own standpoint, was in the right. Rev. Mr. Manning said, if John Brown had consulted him in regard to inciting a slave insurrection he should certainly have advised him not to do it, but he was far from regretting that the attempt had been made. Phillips was the last speaker, and treated his subject in the boldest revolutionary manner; and before he had finished the applause was deafening. A judge of the superior-court sat on the front bench clapping his hands with a noise like pistol shots.

This served him as a preparation for the Brooklyn address already referred to, which, if it had been equal throughout, might be classed among the world's great speeches, and it is certainly one of the most brilliant orations of either ancient or modern times. Certain passages in it remind one of a shower of falling stars. It is remarkable for its light and shade. He began with a gay and graceful compliment to Thomas Corwin, an old statesman of the Henry Clay school, who was seated on the platform; but he soon became intensely serious. "The lesson of the hour is insurrection. And why is it? Because we are all recreant Americans; recreant to the principles of our ancestors." After a while he changed to a sort of rippling humor, which was peculiar to him, and delighted his audience immensely, describing the subterfuges which had come into fashion to escape using the word slavery. "Hypocrisy is the homage that vice pays to virtue." Then he became deeply pathetic as he referred to the heroic man condemned to death and lying wounded in a Virginia prison; and concluded with an outburst of spiritual triumph like that in Goethe's tragedy of Egmont. "They have brave men in Virginia: it was not an old, grey-headed man entering Harper's Ferry that they were afraid of, it was the John Brown in every man's own conscience that made them tremble."

He achieved an equal success of a different kind soon after, in attempting to deliver the same speech in New York city. A portion of the hall was filled with pro-slavery roughs who cursed and reviled him, and threw various missiles at him. A stone which struck a chair near him on the platform might have done him very serious injury. Nothing dismayed, he continued his speech, and taking his text from the insults of his enemies, hurled defiance back in their teeth. His friends who accompanied him and were ready to defend him from personal violence, said that on this occasion Phillips surpassed any thing they had known of him before; and fairly quelled the mob by his courage, address, and personal magnetism.

It was during the following eight years that Wendell Phillips proved himself the great orator. Wasson, who never quite approved of him, said that Webster might have excelled him, but that Choate or Everett could not be compared with him. The largest halls could not contain the people who wished to hear him. He was several times mobbed, and his life was in continual danger. A body-guard of devoted young friends escorted him to and from his house. He never ceased calling for the emancipation of the negroes, and when that was accomplished, for their enlistment as volunteers and a more vigorous prosecution of the war. His criticism of public affairs was not always judicious, but it warmed the hearts of the people and strengthened the hands of the anti-slavery party in Washington. The real difficulty at that time was best known to Lincoln and his cabinet; the difficulty of organizing such large armies with so small a number of trained and experienced officers. Good judges have given an opinion that the practice of appointing noted politicians to important commands lengthened the war at least two years, and one after another, all these men had to be removed; but what else could the government do? The officers of the regular army nearly all belonged to the democratic party, and President

Lincoln hardly knew whom he could trust. Phillips knew as little of military affairs as Grant did of oratory.

Just one year after the Brooklyn address, he was called upon to celebrate the election of Abraham Lincoln in Boston Music Hall. For once Phillips and his audience were in perfect harmony, and also in the best of spirits. Men little dreamed at that time of the awful chasm that was to open beneath them. His speech was full of the most delicious humor; rather a biting humor at times, as we read it now, but it did not seem so in the way he spoke it. It was like a wedding feast: laughter and applause were so frequent that the wonder is that the speaker was able to keep the thread of his discourse. Among a dozen witty passages, he said, "Now I would like to have a law that one-third of our able men should not be eligible for the presidency. Then every third man could be depended on to tell the truth. Listen to Mr. Seward on the prairies; what magnificent speeches he has made there since Mr. Lincoln's nomination. When he ceased to be a candidate for the presidency, he became a man again."

In the winter of 1863 he went to Washington for the first time, and lectured on the lesson of the hour. "Old Abe" went to hear him and expressed himself as being greatly pleased with the exhibition, as he called it. Next day a committee of influential citizens called on him to inquire if he could deliver his oration on "Toussaint" that evening for the benefit of his admirers; and then that was not enough, but they must have his lecture on "The Lost Arts" the evening afterward. This was a fine triumph for him after twenty-five years of social ostracism but his anxiety in regard to the condition of the country, prevented him from enjoying it as he might have.

Meanwhile a storm was preparing for him in the quarter he least expected it. The old abolitionists, whom nobody had thought of since the repeal of the Missouri compromise and who were beginning to feel a good deal neglected, looked upon Phillips now as a deserter from their standard of non-resistance and moral suasion, and perhaps also eyed his brilliant course with some little jealousy. In the spring of 1865 Garrison returned from hoisting the flag at Fort Sumter, fully satisfied that the negroes could be safely trusted in future to the patriarchal care of the central government. Phillips thought otherwise. He argued that the black man still suffered from the effects of slavery; that they were very much at the mercy of their former masters, who would naturally bear them no good-will; that their future political position would depend on the action of Congress and not on the administration; and that it was still advisable for northern friends to keep watch over their interests.

From this private difference of opinion an obstinate controversy soon developed itself, in which a large portion of the public took part on one side or the other. Senator Sumner and his friends supported Phillips; while Governor Andrew, who disliked him for no very good reason, and Senator Wilson for a much better one, supported Garrison. Both parties being thus strongly reinforced, the dispute rose to a high pitch. Phillips finally carried the day, and was fully justified afterwards for doing so; but the Garrison party took mortal offence at him for this, and would never afterwards recognize him except by a cold and distant courtesy. George Thompson, an English friend of Garrison who came over providentially at that time, quoted Phillips' earlier speeches against him (an inconsistency which was rather to his credit) and exclaimed, "I appeal from Phillips drunk to Phillips sober:" nor was this the worst of it. [Footnote: A year after this he said to two Rhode Island ladies, who were among the few friends that remained faithful to him all through life, "It seems hard that of the men whom I worked with for thirty years only three or four are willing to speak to me now."] But Phillips endured the storm like a man. He argued his case with all the ardor and energy of his nature, but there escaped from him not one opprobrious or resentful sentence towards his former associates. Emerson said (to quote him again, and we hope for the last time): "How handsomely Mr. Phillips has behaved in his controversy with Mr. Garrison. In fact Phillips was the same we have always known him." But the wound went deep into him; and seven years later, when he said at the Radical Club, "I have known cases in which it only took *one* to make a quarrel," we all recognized what he was thinking of.

This was the acme of his career, and alas! how soon he fell away from it. About a year before this time, his friends began to notice certain expressions in his speeches which puzzled them not a little. At length a severe and unjust attack on Senator Wilson as a frequenter of drinking-saloons explained the new departure to them. Phillips was evidently taking a hand in practical politics, and as Wilson's term was nearly expiring, wished to make General Butler his successor. So strangely are good and evil united in us, that this happened about the same period as the Garrison controversy. The less said about General Butler perhaps the better. At the same time Wendell Phillips' support of him would seem to be no worse than Judge Hoar's continued support of Blaine for the presidency; and it is also true that General Butler's reputation was better at this time than it afterwards became; he was well received at the political clubs, and even considered in the light of a presidential candidate by prominent republicans. Phillips' subsequent explanation of the matter was, that the negro was his client, and General Butler was the only person who had the will and ability to manage his case.

He was not inconsistent in this, for he afterwards supported General Grant in the machine governments at the south for the same reason.

Another bond of mutual interest between them was socialism. When or where Phillips became a socialist is uncertain. He was conservative in religion, and there is no more necessary connection between the abolition of slavery and socialism than between socialism and free-trade. On the contrary, the votes of the Irish laborers, who now divided his interest with the negroes, had always been the chief bulwark and mainstay of the slave power in the northern states. It must however, have been a question of principle with him, a theory of abstract right, for the course and conduct of his whole life is a true witness against any meaner motive. But General Butler's socialism was doubtless a matter of personal ambition—a bait to catch the popular vote. Nobody except Phillips, not even the laborers themselves, imagined anything else in his case. [Footnote: In the autumn of 1884 my brother asked a plumber then working for him, if he intended to vote for General Butler, who was presidential candidate that year for the labor-party. "No," replied the fellow, "Butler is a bad man; he will do for Governor of Massachusetts, but for President of the United States we want something different."] This unholy alliance was productive of no good to either party: Phillips injured his reputation by it, and what advantage Butler may have gained is yet to be discovered.

In 1870 Phillips injured himself still more by a public attack on the Bird Club; a company of merchants and politicians who met together for a Saturday-afternoon dinner. This was done so evidently in Butler's interest that the general's future plans were disclosed by it. He wished to obtain the nomination for governor the following year, and looked upon the Bird Club as the chief obstacle in the way of his doing so.

Frank W. Bird, who usually presided at the table, was one of the most patriotic and single-minded men that ever labored for the good of his country. He was so sincere and warm-hearted that there was no possibility of mistaking his character. He was in the legislature for nearly twenty years, and a member of the governor's council; but offices were not what he cared for. He was at once the most intimate friend of Andrew and Sumner,—two men who never could agree because one wanted to organize all men under his banner, and the other was equally determined to be independent of everybody. He might almost have been called the balance-wheel of Massachusetts politics. At the State House he was the terror of all mean and mischievous members; a sentinel always on the watch to prevent extravagance, fraud, and political chicanery. His persistent opposition to that monstrous abortion the Houssac tunnel, for which our children and grandchildren will be taxed *ad infinitum*, cost him an election to Congress.

Upon this account he had numerous enemies, but even General Butler could not discover the smallest reproach against his character. He was one of the most useful men in the State. The club was called by his name because it had neither name nor organization. It originated with a few friends who used to meet at Chevalier Howe's office during the Kansas excitement; and Wendell Phillips' charge against them that they managed the politics of Massachusetts, had less than half a leg to stand on. While the governor and both senators were members of the club it must have been of course an influential body. Sumner certainly never made use of official patronage to promote his private interests. Yet this was the only charge, mixed with some dark insinuations, that Phillips could bring against them; and even this might have had some excuse if it had not been in the interest of General Butler.

The remainder of his life was a wreck, though he may not have been aware of it. Frank Bird and his associates were the best friends that Wendell Phillips ever had. They were friends who would have held fast to him through everything except such an attack as he made on them. Alone now with his invalid wife, childless and well-nigh friendless, his life must have been gloomy and miserable. No company was ever invited to his house, and it was by the rarest chance that he went to any entertainment. Who his associates were in this new phase of his life, is often a matter of conjecture. Revolutionary socialists mostly, practical and unpractical—not of the harmless theoretical sort: but he never was seen on the street in company with other men. Whoever they were, they could not have been either cheerful or elevating society. The audiences that went to hear him were composed of quite a different class of people from those of the preceding era, and could not sustain him with the same moral force as formerly. No wonder if his temper became sharp and his mind melancholic; if the lines deepened in his face and the quick, bright look of his eye changed to a fitful, suspicious and desperate expression; if his splendid talent deteriorated too much into mannerism. Although this was his own fault, we could not help feeling pity for him, and the kind of regret with which we look on the fragments of a beautiful statue. He was evidently carried away with the ambition of becoming a world reformer.

There is a sentence in his speech on Lincoln's election which may cast light on Wendell Phillips' socialistic views. He says, "Caesar crossed the Rubicon borne in the arms of a people trodden into poverty and chains by an oligarchy of slaveholders; but that oligarchy proved too strong even for

Caesar and his legions." This was a bold and original opinion in those days, for Mommsen's history, to which we are mainly indebted for our change of sentiment in regard to Caesar, had not yet been translated. There is at the present time an oligarchy of land owners and capitalists in England of whom Froude has predicted that they will come to the same catastrophe as the Roman oligarchy did finally, and as that of Bohemia in the sixteenth century, and of France in the eighteenth, unless the present course of events shall be arrested by judicious legislation and magnanimous sacrifices. Phillips had already taken a hand in suppressing one American oligarchy, who have been compared by Mommsen to the Roman senatorial party, and he thought he foresaw another rising in our midst from the iron kings, and other great industrial magnates. He may have been far-sighted in this, for he often proved to be a true prophet, and there are many now who think the same; but that would not justify the methods by which he undertook to provide against the evil. The condition of the laboring classes in America, where a thrifty and temperate mechanic can occupy as good a house as a country doctor in Europe, is the most favorable yet known in history; much more favorable, comparatively, than that of our professional classes; but Phillips had seen the most wealthy and highly educated people ranged against him throughout the long conflict with slavery, and had acquired the habit of considering them a dangerous element in the community.

There is a certain artistic perfection in the contrasts of his life. Thirty-seven years after his Lovejoy speech, he appeared again in Faneuil Hall attended by a retinue of government employees, with intent to capture a meeting called to protest against the interference of the government at Washington in Louisiana politics. There was wrong no doubt on both sides of this question, but the interference of the government was equally illegal and injudicious. Phillips appeared now more on the side of the oppressor than for the oppressed, and though his speech was, as formerly, the best of the occasion, it failed to win the sympathy of the audience. He was consistent in his devotion to the interests of the freed, men, but he would have been more true to himself if he had been willing to recognize, as the more reasonable anti-slavery people did, how absurd and even abominable, were the negro governments in the southern states; but he had long since lost his good judgment, and when President Hayes removed the troops for whose maintenance he could obtain no appropriation from Congress, and the pyramid which had been so long supported on its apex suddenly fell over, Phillips could scarcely find terms harsh enough to express his rage and exasperation. His attacks on the Hayes administration might fairly be called philippics had they possessed the saving grace of Hellenic self-control, but they remind us rather of Carlyle's furious "Latter Day Pamphlets."

Yet even in December there are bright days, and when in his seventieth year the veteran orator was invited to deliver an address before the graduates of his own college, from whose festivities he had been excluded since the time of his Lovejoy speech, warmed with the recollections of his youth, his genius blazed forth with all its former brilliancy. With customary hardihood he selected for his subject "The Danger from the Educated Classes"; that is, the tendency of intellectual culture to exclusiveness and separation from the less fortunate portion of mankind. It is not to be supposed that the Harvard Alumni were well pleased with this topic, but he presented it with so much skill, and even eloquence, as to win applause from some of his most inveterate opponents. This sympathy for the unfortunate had been the key-note and true explanation of his course in life. It came to him there in the days of his youthful gayety like a dream, and now after fifty years he had returned to celebrate his last triumph in the same place where this vision of Heavenly mercy had appeared to him.

He looked like Cicero, and there is a bust of Cicero on the Pincian hill at Rome, which if placed in Boston would certainly be mistaken for him. His figure, however, was better than Cicero's, who is reported to have had a long neck and rather slender legs. He resembled Cicero in his refined tastes, his admiration for great writers his command of language, his tact, fluency, fiery invective, and in the anti-climax of his career. If he had prepared his speeches for a body of men like the Roman senate, he might have been more nearly Cicero's equal. He used to wear a high-crowned soft felt hat, which was remarkably suited to the Roman-like contour of his face. He was skillful in all things, and might have been equally celebrated as a writer, an actor, or possibly as an artist, if his interest and inclination had led him in either of these directions. What we feel the lack of in him is contemplative depth: he was more Gallic than Germanic. He possessed a deep nature, but his character was not equal to it. He was too refined, too much of an artist perhaps, for the rough work fortune gave him to do. He had the heart of a lion, but the mind of a woman.

Yet as we view his life from a distance it has grand outlines. When the western continent was discovered, it seemed as if it were a paradise which had been kept in reserve for the most civilized races; but this had no sooner happened, than a curse was fastened upon it,—the curse of slavery, which had already been abolished in Europe in its mildest type. This may have been necessary at first in the tropical portions of America, where it is impossible for a white man to labor in the sun; but it was contrary to the spirit of Christianity and inimical to true civilization. To eradicate this wide-spread, deep-rooted evil was a tremendous undertaking, one of the most gigantic in history; and among those who contributed to this, none, except perhaps John Brown and Charles Sumner, accomplished more—and few have done so much as Wendell Phillips. The right aspect then in which to regard his career, is as a sacrifice to this great cause. Let it be said of him that he loved mankind not wisely, but too well.

APPLEDORE AND THE LAIGHTONS

The Isles of Shoals are seven: Duck, Appledore, Cedar, Haley's, Star, Londoner's, and White. Besides these there are Square Rock, Mingo Rock, and a number of other out-lying rocks and reefs. Appledore, Haley's, Cedar, Star, and Londoner's form almost a semi-circle, or horse-shoe, nearly a mile in width with the tips turned toward the west. Duck Island lies a mile-and-a-half to the north of this group, and White Island with it's light-house about the same distance to the south-east.

They are mostly bare rocks, like mountain tops rising above the water. They are not however submerged mountains, for as their name indicates the sea is nowhere very deep about them. If the points of the horse-shoe had been turned toward the east instead of the west they would not have been habitable and the place would have been known to navigators as the Devil's Reef, the Devil's Horse-shoe or by some other term ominous of shipwrecks. The group of islands now form a cosy though not very safe harbor where every evening in the mackerel season a small fleet of fishing-vessels sail in there to anchor for the night.

As might be expected the fauna and flora of the Shoals is neither rare nor extensive. Gulls are to be seen of course at all times,—especially the large burgomaster gull, one of the finest of birds in size and ferocity, and in power of sight nearly equal to an eagle. In spring and fall flocks of coot and the more fishy sort of ducks are to be found there together with a good many loons. Snowy owls are not uncommon in cold weather, and during winter almost any kind of Arctic bird may arrive there. A flock of eider ducks once took refuge and were shot under the same overhanging rock where the terrified servant-girl concealed herself when pursued by the murderer Wagner. There are probably more green snakes on Appledore than anywhere else in America. Wild roses and morning-glories are the only flowers large enough to attract the notice of a passing tourist, but Celia Thaxter has also written a pretty poem on the pimpernel. There are no trees to speak of.

Their geological structure is more interesting. It is generally supposed that the soil of New England rests on a foundation of primeval granite, but it is not exactly that. There is very little true granite in New England, what is taken for it commonly being syenite, a rock indeed that differs from granite only in the substitution of hornblend for mica. The so-called Quincy granite is a finer sort of syenite, and the White Mountains are composed of syenite capped with granite. The Isles of Shoals are also mostly syenite, but there are large boulders of coarse granite lying about, and in some places the syenite changes suddenly to granite as if the two had been welded together. Then there are dykes of dark brown trap or ancient lava, from four to ten feet wide running across the islands from south-west to north-east, and others again at right-angles to these. This would seem to indicate that the elevation above the surrounding plateau was due to volcanic action. The structure of White Island is very different from the others, a large portion of the rock being studded with innumerable small garnets, while veins of some grayish white minerals run through it in which there are still smaller garnets.

How did these bare, bleak and barren rocks come to be inhabited? Originally it was from love of gold. Men will go wherever there is money to be made, and wherever men go women are pretty sure to follow. In 1879 a city suddenly arose in the most desolate and uncomfortable part of the Rocky Mountains; and in the middle of the last century there was a large settlement on the Isles of Shoals, with a young ladies' boarding-school at Appledore, and a fort on Star Island for protection against pirates and Indians. Fish merchants carried on a flourishing trade with France and Spain. In course of time however cod and haddock became largely fished out and the settlement on Appledore disappeared with them, boarding-school and all. So it is predicted that some day Leadville will again become a silent wilderness. In 1850 the population of the Shoals had dwindled to about a dozen families of poor fishermen when a fresh impulse was given to the activity of the place from a direction that nobody could ever have imagined.

The Laightons were residents of Portsmouth. The father of Thomas B. Laighton was a spar-maker and did a considerable business when shipbuilding was thriving in those times. Thomas B. in his youth was afflicted with a fever which confined him to his room for many months and from the effects of which he never recovered. He married Miss Eliza Rymes, a woman of remarkable good-sense and strong physique. He preferred journalism to spar-making, and his connection with the New Hampshire Gazette soon led him into politics. He was an ardent supporter of "old Hickory" and rewarded for it finally with the position of postmaster for his native city. Whether he surrendered this position for the forlorn and less lucrative one of White Island lighthouse on account of ill-health or from a different motive, is uncertain. There was formerly a story in circulation that he was defeated as a candidate for some political office and retired in disgust from the haunts and ways of men. This however is not likely. Thomas Laighton was a man of a blunt and rugged sincerity, tenacious and determined; such as would not be likely to lose his mental balance at the first unfavorable turn of fortune.

He went to White Island in 1838, was removed by Harrison the First and reappointed by Tyler. His life there must have been a rough one. Of all the Isles of Shoals, White Island is the most difficult of access. It is not easy to land there in good summer weather, and during winter communication with the outer world is as rare as cold days in July. From December till May the breakers thunder on the cliff beneath the light-house like the roar of artillery. One would like to know what his reflections may have been during this Alexander Selkirk kind of life,—how he and his wife managed to entertain themselves. Rev. John Weiss and a friend going to Portsmouth in the summer of '46 visited the lighthouse and made friends with the family there. They found old Laighton a pretty rough customer, but good humored enough, and his wife uncommonly glad to see them. Their daughter Celia was a very bright looking, rosy faced girl, and the two boys Oscar and Cedric had their hair cut straight across their foreheads to keep it out of their eyes. Mr. Weiss thought that when they were in the water they must have looked a good deal like seals.

In 1848 he resigned his position and removed to Appledore; then as always on the charts of the coast-survey known as Hog Island. It would seem to be the last stretch of a fisherman's imagination to call every long sloping island by that name. There he and his brother Joseph, who had thus far been a grocer in Portsmouth, built cottages for themselves and went into the fishing business, purchasing boats, seines, and hiring a large number of men. This lasted for some years and finally came to an end through the death of Joseph and the invalidism of Thomas, who was always lame and unable to give the work his personal supervision. Meanwhile their friends came over from the mainland to visit them, and admired the climate so much and remained so long that the brothers concluded to build a small hotel where these and others could pay for their entertainment. It was a three-story building, almost square, the parent stem of that great banyan-tree which has since spread over a large portion of the island. The accomodations at first were primitive. A visitor in '51 was obliged to wait an hour for a room and an opportunity to wash his hands, though he was at the time the only guest in the house. An empty flour-barrel turned upside down served for a wash-stand. However, the sailing and fishing were good, as also were Mrs. Laighton's doughnuts, of which there was always an unfailing supply, so that numbers of people came there.

Among them was a recent graduate of Harvard, from the vicinity of Boston, named Levi Thaxter. He was a young man of refined tastes and rare intellectual endowment; afterwards widely known as the apostle of Browning's poetry in America. He was not one of those college graduates who seemed to have been run in a mould like bullets, but already possessed character and a mind of his own. He was by nature rather an admirer of art than an artist; in fact he was a critic, and with a right opportunity he might have become a Froude, a Taine, or a Ruskin. A wise father might have done much for him, but his father belonged to that class of men who are only acquainted with a small circle of their own affairs; he had not the least conception of what was needed for his brilliant son. So the best years of young Thaxter's life were consumed in fruitless efforts to harmonize his lofty aspirations with the stubborn facts about him. It was like a fruit-tree planted in a stone quarry. Too late he learned from experience the wisdom that should have come to him from his ancestors. He might have succeeded better if he had been less unwilling to compromise his sincerity,—to duck his head to the golden calf. But he would not do that, he intended to remain Levi Thaxter or die in the attempt: and once he came very near doing so. He was a romance character, and if his biography could be written it would be more interesting than that of some of our most celebrated men. Socially he was delightful; and a hundred friends could bear witness to his integrity, his fidelity, his kindly nature, his wit, humor, and keen appreciation. William Hunt the painter and Doctor Henry I. Bowditch were his two most intimate friends.

He studied dramatic reading, and nearly made a profession of it. Actors sometimes studied with him to learn a good pronunciation and dramatic effect. His partiality for Browning's poetry is quite generally known. He first read it to his friends; then in private companies; and finally in public halls. When in 1882 he went to Philadelphia to read Browning there he created such enthusiasm for the subject that the libraries and bookstores were quickly exhausted and fresh copies of Browning had to be sent for from other cities to supply the demand. He considered Browning, Aeschylus and Shakespeare the three most dramatic writers. All the Browning clubs that have nourished so extensively for many years past might be considered Levi Thaxter's lineal descendants.

His conversation on art and literature was often so interesting that it is a pity his occasional bursts of eloquence could not have been preserved. But the important matter at this moment is that he fell in love with Celia Laighton, married her and carried her off to the environs of Boston, where she made valuable friends and met with larger opportunities for intellectual development.

Hawthorne came to the Shoals on the thirtieth of August, 1852, and has given a full account of his visit in his usual minute and pictorial manner. He left Franklin Pierce, who was then candidate for the presidency, in Concord, New Hampshire, and embarked at Portsmouth in a small schooner which was then the only mode of conveyance,—-and often a very dilatory one. On the way two of his fellow passengers became sea-sick, and another "sat in the stern looking very white." On arriving at Appledore he was met in the doorway by Mr. Laighton of whom he gives rather a realistic description; adding, however, "He addressed me in a hearty, hospitable tone, and judging that it must be my landlord, I delivered a letter of introduction from Pierce, which of course gave me the best the house afforded."

It seems strange that Hawthorne, who understood human nature better than any other American writer, should have so rarely penetrated into the character of the people whom he mentions in his note-books. Old Laighton was a solid rock of sense and grit, and the chief impression he made upon strangers was of a man whom it was best to keep on the right side of. The detonations of his frankness sometimes cleared the air in a truly remarkable manner, and would scatter all light spirits to a prudent distance. He reminded one of Longfellow's description of Simon Danz:

> "Restless at times with heavy strides
> He paces his parlor to and fro;
> He is like a ship that at anchor rides,
> And swings with the rising and falling tides,
> And tugs at her anchor-tow."

Hawthorne seems to have found a kindred spirit in Mr. Thaxter, who invited him to their cottage to meet the ladies and drink apple-jack. There he also found John Weiss, a man of wit and genius little inferior to his own. Neither did Celia Thaxter impress him, except in a rather external way. He says, "We found Mrs. Thaxter sitting in a neat little parlor, very simply furnished, but in good taste. She is not now, I believe, more than eighteen years old, very pretty, and with the manners of a lady,—not prim and precise, but with enough of freedom and ease."

The ideality in her face, which probably attracted her husband and is visible in her earliest pictures, was not observed by the idealist himself. He spent the next two weeks in company with Mr. Thaxter, roaming about on the water, visiting different islands, and conversing with the inhabitants. It must have been a rare occasion for young Thaxter, and Hawthorne for once found a companion who could either be silent or talk in an interesting manner. Hawthorne's account of it would suffice as a guide-book for the Shoals. He tells the story of Betty Moody, who was said to have concealed herself with her baby in a sort of cave on Star Island in order to escape from the Indians who had made a raid on the place while her husband was fishing out at sea. Unhappily the child screamed, and the wretched mother is said to have murdered it to prevent discovery. How the other wives and mothers on the island saved themselves at this juncture is not reported; and the myth no doubt originated from a dark red lichen growing on the rocks there which resembles blood-stains and has a scientific name to that effect.

Much more probable is the tradition that a large heap of stones formed like an Esquimaux hut on the highest point of Appledore, was built there by Captain John Smith and his men as a memorial of their discovery of the islands. This heap of stones is a veritable cairn, such as climbers of the Alps build on the summits of those peaks which they have ascended for the first time. It is customary in such cases to insert a champagne bottle among the stones, containing the card of the fortunate explorer; but perhaps Captain Smith was not provided with these articles while cruising off the coast of North America. It is at least more interesting and more in keeping with the rugged aspect of the place than the delicate triangular plinth that has been erected to his memory on Star Island. Another poetic subject is the Spaniards' graves on Smutty Nose: hapless mariners, wrecked where no friendly or kindred eye will look on the cold stones which mark their interment!

Eleven years elapsed before Hawthorne visited the Shoals again, and for the last time in his life. Meanwhile much had changed there. The hotel had grown by the addition of a large dormitory; and the boys, Oscar and Cedric, had grown up with it to be vigorous and very healthy looking young men. The Hon. Thomas P. Laighton had become a confirmed invalid; nor did he live very long after this time. The management of the property was wholly in the hands of his sons. Mrs. Thaxter had grown to a bright, self-possessed woman with three small boys to look after, and with her reputation as a poet now well assured to her both by critics and the general public. Her face, figure and manner all gave evidence of a concentrated personality. Her husband, a handsome and full-bearded man, was now in the prime of life and intellectual vigor. Rev. John Weiss, their never-failing friend and a constant habitue of the place, had written the life of Theodore Parker, and received due recognition as a gifted man and elegant speaker. And there was another, more distinguished than them all,—a tall figure, more erect than a soldier, pacing across the long piazza, or watching a game in the billiard-room, or seated in a retired corner of Mrs. Thaxter's parlor, whose face had long since been known to Hawthorne as that of John G. Whittier.

Social life at the Shoals has had its incipient childhood, its period of youthful strength and gaiety, its bright noontide of maturity, and seems now to be lapsing into a serene and comfortable old age. Many, at least, of the brilliant men and women who made it what it was, are gone, and others do not appear to take their places. The Isles of Shoals are changing as all things change except the rocks and sea. The south-easterly parlor in Mrs. Thaxter's cottage is historic ground. "There have been fine people here," she said one day in September, about ten years ago, as the house was closing for the season, "but the summer is gone, and they have gone with it." Nowhere else since Margaret Fuller's time have so many wits, geniuses and brilliant women been gathered together. Whittier and Hawthorne are enough to have consecrated it, but there have been many others. Hunt, the painter, came there, and Professor Paine, the composer, as well as other fine artists and musicians. Even Ole Bull, that Norwegian waif and celebrated violinist, wandered in there of a forenoon, and entertained the company with accounts of sea-serpents standing on their tails in front of water-falls, and other marvels only visible in Norway:—supposing, I presume, that his hearers would believe anything that he told them.

Mrs. Thaxter's poetry, like all genuine poetry, is indigenous,—native to the soil. She has taken her subjects from the life and incidents about her: the little sand-piper, the burgomaster gull, the pimpernel, and the wreck on White Island—where a vessel was once wrecked in a dense fog right under the light-house. [Footnote: In the winter of 1876, centennial year, a schooner laden with salt somehow ran on to the southerly reef of White Island and lost its rudder. The vessel consequently became unmanageable, and was finally thrown up on Londoner's, where the island is so low that at high tide the sea nearly divides it in two. The crew tried to escape by jumping on to the rocks. Only three succeeded in doing this, the captain, the cabin-boy and one sailor, A tremendous wave washed over them, and when it had subsided the sailor found himself alone. Fortunately he knew where he was, and by clinging flat to the rocks, like a starfish, and watching his chances, he succeeded after a time in reaching a point of safety. But no sooner was he fairly out of the water than his clothes became a mass of ice. There is a rude, unplastered house on Londoner's. The door was fastened, but he broke through it with a blow of his foot, then wiping his hands as well as he could on the rough boards, he felt along the first transverse beam-joist until, to his great delight, he came upon some matches. These saved his life, for there can be no doubt that otherwise he would have been frozen to death before morning. There was a stove in the house, and even a few sticks of wood. For kindling-wood he tore off splinters from the edges of the boards. He could see nothing within the house, and it is said that after his fire was lighted, he had only one match left. Next morning people on Haley's Island saw the wreck and the smoke from his fire, and went to his rescue.

Mrs. Rymes is authority for the statement that White Island was not called so from its color, but from a family of Whites who lived on it before the light-house was built, and that the miser White who was murdered by Crowninshield in Salem was born on that island.]

She made the best use of her material, which after all is much the same as Emerson's, with the difference between a barren island and a well-wooded country town taken into account. Another difference is that she looks at her subject objectively, and then treats it subjectively; whereas Emerson does exactly the reverse. It is like the difference between Schiller and Goethe, or Longfellow and Browning; and is the manner in which a poet always must write in order to be popular. Her verses are graceful, refined, and—as they should be—feminine. Yet there is a good deal of strength in it also: or if the phrase is permissible, a good deal of back-bone.

Her style reminds one of Whittier, but is sufficiently original. Sometimes she escapes from concrete things into abstract subjects; and her short poem on "Heroism" seems to me the best she ever wrote. There was formerly a strong prejudice against this kind of poetry, but it seems to be disappearing. Those of her poems which Whittier included in his collection of English and American poetry are also fine, and may be said to deserve their place. Her criticism was better than is usually the case with poets; and her conversation about authors and literature always interesting. It was not didactic at all, but frank, spontaneous and open to correction. She liked the most diverse writers; Tennyson, and Dickens, and Browning. In early years I remember her speaking of Hawthorne in a tone of veneration; but later in life she preferred Emerson, even to Whittier. There was formerly a portrait of Goethe in her parlor with Emerson's lines about him underneath it, copied in her own picturesque hand-writing.

It seems strange that she never tried her hand at a novel, for of all resorts on the coast the Isles of Shoals is the best ground to study human nature on. People lose their artificial ways in that atmosphere and their peculiarities are brought out distinctly, as oil brings out the veins in black walnut. The epic gift, however, is very different from the lyric and the two are not often united in the same person. Mrs. Thaxter's prose writings are almost as rare as Whittier's. She published a detailed account of a murder that was committed on Haley's Island about twenty years ago;—what would seem to be a peculiar subject for a cultivated person to fasten on—and yet she succeeded in giving it a good deal of dignity. One consequence of this has been that hundreds of people cross over every summer to Smutty Nose to stare at the miserable old shanty where the event took place, though there is absolutely nothing to be seen there.

It was a choice occasion in the old Shoals days when Mrs. Thaxter consented to read Browning or Tennyson to her friends. I think it was the finest reading I ever heard, simply because it was neither dramatic, rhetorical, nor elocutionary. It was plain, distinct reading with just enough of the dramatic element to give fullness to the meaning,—and with such a voice! Why is it that some people who have unpleasant voices are yet able to sing sweetly, and others who cannot sing are able to read or converse so it is music to hear them? I was formerly acquainted with an old man, much beyond the period of life when singers retire from the stage, whose voice was nevertheless, as one heard it at some distance, as musical as a Stradivarius.

With all her frankness and fearlessness, she was as sensitive to personal influences as poets usually are; and persons who called on her, who lacked delicacy of feeling, not only wearied her, but sometimes caused her positive suffering. In such cases she fortified herself with what she called a strong dose of conversation; would talk with great volubility on all possible subjects, as if in this manner to keep the unpleasant influence at a distance. "I wish all good people," she said, "were pleasant, and all the bad people disagreeable; for then life would be a more simple affair than it is now. The world is such a mixture that I never quite know how to take it."

At times she was a merciless critic. An admiring Quaker in Philadelphia wrote some verses in honor of Whittier, which were presented to Mrs. Thaxter for her approval. When she was asked how she liked them, she replied, "I do not like it all; it goes humpety, lumpety, dumpety, bump;" and immediately changed the subject of conversation.

On another occasion she took up a volume of poetry which had been printed for private circulation, and said, "There are two really fine poems in this, which is more than can be usually said of such collections." Then she read them to us with such expressive grace as might almost make poetry out of Latin grammar. One was called the "Whip of the Sky," and the other was a sonnet about Pompeii.

She early discovered in herself the mesmeric power of a spiritist; and Wasson was present at a *seance* which she gave at the house of a friend in Newburyport, reporting messages from another world to various persons in the room. She thus naturally became a believer in spiritism, and finally a Theosophist; but she found that such supernatural performances were physically injurious and mentally demoralizing, so that in later years she rarely indulged in them.

One cold, foggy evening in August, 1868, we were gathered in the parlor of the Thaxter cottage, when some one proposed that we should make an experiment with planchette. So the little triangular board was produced, with a long pencil in the apex, and a large sheet of brown paper. Mrs. Thaxter placed her left hand on it, and Mrs. H., a New York lady, placed her right hand, while the rest of us formed a circle around the table.

In five or ten minutes, planchette began to move, and wrote out "John Laighton," in plain, bold letters. "He was my great-uncle," said Mrs. Thaxter; "and there used to be a proverb in Portsmouth, 'As honest as John Laighton.'" Then she wrote on the paper: "Where is my father?"

A few minutes afterward, Mrs. H. closed her eyes, and fell back in her chair, as if she were fainting. Suddenly coming to herself, she seized the pencil from planchette and wrote rapidly on the paper, while Mrs. Thaxter held her other hand. She was at the left of Mrs. Thaxter, but I cannot remember now whether Mrs. H. wrote with her right or left hand. Mrs. Thaxter was greatly excited and looked all the time in Mrs. H.'s face in the most earnest and impressive manner. Mrs. H. behaved like a person under the influence of strong emotion, and continued to write intermittently until the sheet of paper was nearly covered. Mrs. Thaxter read the sentences eagerly, but without saying a word. Several times Mr. H. entreated his wife to desist, but she paid no attention to him. The whole performance lasted nearly half an hour, and when it was over, Mrs. Thaxter said, "They are all answers to questions which I asked of my father," and remained very grave and quiet during the rest of the evening.

The next forenoon we examined the paper and found the writing on it was intelligible, but at the same time conveyed no real information. They were such answers as a woman might herself suggest to a person who was slow in making a reply. One of them was, "You will know everything perfectly when the right time comes." Mr. H. said, "My wife never could have imagined all this; there must have been some occult communication between her and Mrs. Thaxter. Neither do I think she ever heard before of John Laighton." Mrs. Thaxter evidently was satisfied that she had received messages from her father, who had been dead about two years; and though the rest of us did not credit this, the fact in itself seemed marvellous enough.

When some one remarked that he would give five dollars at any time to see a ghost, Mrs. Thaxter retorted, "I think you would give fifty to have him leave you again."

Where the poetical talent of the Laighton family came from is a rare mystery. Both of Mrs. Thaxter's brothers inherited a share of it. A poem of Oscar's was published in the "Atlantic" many years ago, and afterwards included in her first volume of poetry. Cedric wrote a very amusing parody on his sister's "Little Sandpiper," and sent it to her when she was staying in Boston. The scene was represented in winter when there wasn't any little sandpiper.

Mrs. Thaxter's poetry, however, was the making of Appledore as a summer resort. Between 1865 and 1875 thousands of people came there every summer to catch a sight of her. How she dared to go to the dinner-table in the face of such a multitude, I do not know; but after a time she retained a body-guard of friends, old and young, who were quite sufficient to keep intruders at a distance; and they could not be prevented from walking around her cottage, peering in at the windows, and stealing an occasional flower from her garden. Some even walked boldly into her parlor to demand an autograph. She received strange letters also from her unknown admirers. One was from a woman who wished to come to see her, but was afraid to do so on account of the green snakes which Hawthorne speaks of as inhabiting Appledore. (Hawthorne accidentally caught one of these pretty reptiles by the tail, and was not a little startled by it.) Another was from a naval officer who had been forcibly retired to a plantation in Maryland. I suppose she was secretly pleased by this rude homage of the vulgar, but no one knew better that the approval of her friends Weiss and Whittier was worth the whole of it.

Meanwhile social life at Appledore had risen to a height. Mrs. Thaxter welcomed every one who had a claim upon her recognition. Open table was her motto, rather than exclusiveness; but those who considered themselves of superior clay found no chairs to sit on in her parlor. Her cottage was a scene of gaiety by day, and revelry at night. Beautiful girls, charming women, and distinguished men dazzled the beholder. Singing and laughter as well as instrumental music could often be heard there at a late hour. There are no people who are so full of good spirits in vacation as clergymen and college-professors—it is the reaction from their well-sustained gravity during the remainder of the year—and there was no lack of either.

Among them all none was so brilliant as John Weiss, though Eichberg the violinist came pretty close to him. Both were German Jews; Weiss, however, having been born in America. He belonged to the same type of men as James Russell Lowell and David A. Wasson. He was the friend of both and equal to either in genius. He was the most eloquent preacher in New England at that time, and as a humorist only second to Lowell, if indeed second to any. His wit and his preaching were not, however, of a popular character: something more than phlegmatic common-sense was required to appreciate them. If he was not so popular as Lowell with the public, he was more so among his friends, in whose list might be counted almost every man of note and influence in Boston and vicinity. Bright flashes of his imagination came like the sudden gleam of a diamond, and would often convulse the company with laughter when one would least have expected it.

He was an excellent pantomimist; could perform all the parts in a comedy himself, and with the help of Fred Loring, or some other, would improvise a burlesque on almost any well-known play. It was after one of these performances that Whittier (who sat in his quiet corner enjoying it as much as an honest Quaker dared to) said to Mrs. Thaxter, "Celia, thou knowest I have never been to the theatre, but I think at last the theatre has come to me." Weiss was gay with the gay, but could be profoundly serious again at a moment's warning, and the biting shafts of his satire never wounded a human soul.

When some one spoke of the peculiarity of John Brown's spelling he exclaimed: "So much the better, so much the better! What good would a Webster's dictionary have been at Harper's Ferry? A whole edition of them could not have accomplished anything."

He was always ailing, and his friends in college doubted if he would ever reach maturity; yet he lived to be a grey-haired man, and published a number of excellent books. When he died, in 1878, there were not wanting malicious people to spread the report that he died of intemperance, though the wonder is how he could have lived so long. His death cast a shadow over the social life at Appledore so that it never quite recovered its former gaiety. About the same time several millionaires made their appearance; cottages began to arise upon the rocks; a small steam-yacht plied like a water-bug between the different islands, and the place became continually more fashionable and conventional. Whittier, feeling that he did not belong to this new order of things, retired to a quiet little inn at West Ossipee, in the White Mountains.

It was now that Professor John K. Paine, the musical composer, introduced a new element into the Shoals life. One morning he walked into Mrs. Thaxter's parlor with a large folio under his arm and said, "I am going to play you one of Beethoven's sonatas, for I think you will like it." Mrs. Thaxter was not quite sure that she would, but listened attentively. There had been a good deal of music before, in a small way; pupils of Eichberg playing on the violin with piano accompaniment, and even Eichberg himself,— which was quite a treat, though a single violin can never express a wide range of musical ideas. Beethoven's music she had also heard indifferently performed by young lady amateurs; but this was another affair.

Professor Paine is rather an organist than a pianist, and does not pretend to rare technical skill; but what is much better, he understands the music as only players like Rubinstein and Von Bulow can understand it, and he brought out the meaning with such joyous fullness as even the master himself might have been pleased to hear. It was a revelation to Celia Thaxter: it was easy to see there was no affectation in her enjoyment; neither did she lack words to express her delight. "Mr. Paine," said a classical gentleman who was present, "your playing reminds me of what Cicero said of Caesar's Commentaries, that a fool might think he could improve on it, but a wise man would not like to try." The Professor was so much pleased with Mrs. Thaxter's frank enthusiasm, that he dedicated a sonata he was composing to her, which was performed the following winter in Boston, and greatly praised also by the critics.

Piano recitals and concertos thus became the fashion at Appledore, and classical music was in good demand. Its refining and quieting influence on the little community was quite perceptible. It produced a change like the transition from flamboyant Gothic architecture to the pure Grecian style. At first only a few came to hear it: then the parlor was filled. The piazza became crowded, and finally gentlemen were obliged to find places on the rocks outside.

It is one thing to hear music in a crowded concert-room with gas-light and bad air just after we have left the jarring discords of the street; and quite a different affair to listen to it with congenial spirits in the summer air of these islands, which seems to have been made for attuning the senses to fine perceptions. To enjoy any kind of art, the mind needs to be like a clean slate on which every mark tells.

In 1881 Professor Paine improved his good reputation both here and in Europe by composing what is called his Greek music; that is, an overture to the play of "Oedipus Tyrannus," which was acted at Harvard in the spring of that year. Of course his seashore friends wished to hear him play it himself, and after the applause which followed had subsided, he said: "A little approbation is all the reward I get for my compositions. A good deal of money was made out of the Greek play by speculators, but none of it came to me." There was a general expression of regret; and then Mrs. Thaxter said, as if to herself, "If I were only the Commonwealth of Massachusetts I know what I would do." A physician at the house that summer warned Mrs. Paine never to let her husband work so hard again as he had that year.

I remember William Hunt, the portrait painter, in 1872 wheeling his youngest child, a beautiful boy named Paul, in a go-cart in front of the cottage. He looked like an Arab, with a beard nearly to his waist, and a decidedly Semitic head; but he had an aristocratic style, and the air of a man who was used to command. His friends congratulated themselves on his resemblance to Titian, and to the French artist Horace Vernet. Despite his proud bearing he was a tender-hearted man, and when in trouble always went to Levi Thaxter, who was a rarely sympathetic person. In 1879 he came again to the Shoals, flying from domestic affliction. He was also suffering from a severe nervous strain, the result of painting two immense pictures in the hall of the New York Assembly, at Albany; and was no longer able to work. Either of these by itself he might have contended against, but both together were too much for him.

One dark, rainy night he left the Thaxter cottage at a late hour, looking very sad and gloomy. The next morning his body was found in a freshwater cistern which had been built in a hollow between the rocks. There were some who thought that his death might have been accidental, but old Doctor Bowditch said, "My friends, there was only too much reason for it." Of all the wrecks on that dangerous coast was not this the most piteous and tragical! William Hunt narrowly missed being one of the greatest of painters. Though some of his portraits are wretched failures, there are others of his pictures that might grace any gallery in Europe.

Mountain air is better than sea air, both for those who are well and strong, and generally speaking for invalids; but people go to the sea because they like it,—for love of the dark blue ocean. Few things are more monotonous than sailing in a yacht. It is a confining sort of existence, subjects of conversation soon become exhausted, there are many inconveniences about it, and being becalmed in a ground swell is worse than riding in a stage coach on a hot and dusty road; yet how many men prefer spending their summer vacation in this manner to any other. It is that rolling, lisping, gurgling, mysterious, unfathomable unity which attracts them. Earth is the masculine element, sea the feminine; and all the cycles and epicycles of organic nature have resulted from these two. It develops imagination and romance in persons who would never have been suspected of possessing either. No wonder that the sailor delights in marvelous tales. It is a terrible destroyer, but at the same time a friend that we cannot do without.

Nowhere perhaps is that closeness to the ocean, this familiarity with the sea, so strongly felt as at the Isles of Shoals. There is really no land there: nothing but sky, rock and water. Living there is like a sea-voyage without the discomforts thereof. During the great storm of March '52, when the lighthouse on Minot's Ledge was overturned, an immense wave rolled across the centre of Appledore from side to side. There are windows in the hotel on Star Island where one can drop a pebble into the sea, and go to sleep listening to the murmur of the waves. Even in summer the surf sometimes runs so high that it is dangerous to approach the edge of the cliffs; and few people know how pleasant it is to watch the eddying swirl of the water round the promontories on the westerly side. One can sail in every direction, and if the wind does not suit one quarter it always will another. Better than any sailing, however, is rowing in an open boat at sunset or by moonlight, with one or two friends.

Their climate is equally remarkable, and Doctor Bowditch considered it, from its soothing and also stimulating quality, one of the finest in the world, and much the best on the Atlantic coast. This is owing to their geographical position, islands on the coast of Maine being afflicted with cold fogs, and those south of Cape Cod with warm ones. There are no sultry nights in summer, and the cutting east-winds of Mount Desert are unknown there. The climate is warmer in April and November than on the mainland; in May and October about the same. The winters are disagreeable enough; but there is a kind of glory there in summer, and the view at night from the piazza of the Oceanic is beautiful beyond all faculty of description.

WHITTIER

From under the north star's beam,
Through a region wild and free,
The waters of a mighty stream
Roll onward to the sea.

In the deep clefts of the mountain,
Lie never melting snows;
And there from an icy fountain
A clear cold torrent flows.

When we go to see the Falls of Niagara, we expect to be astonished, and are not disappointed; though the expectation takes away somewhat from our sensation. The grand phenomenon makes a strong and permanent impression on us, and yet there is no feeling of affection mingled with this. We have seen it once and do not care to visit the place again. Many pictures have been painted of it, but they are not genuine pictures, for the human element is wanting in them. Niagara can turn no mill-wheels, and will float no ships. How different is it with those scenes of natural beauty which we never heard of and come upon by surprise—which we remember always with affection and a kindred interest.

Such were my thoughts many years ago at Amesbury, as I walked on the banks of the Merrimac and watched the calm, clear current of the river, as it hastened by, irresistible as time itself. I also reflected how often the poet Whittier must have walked in that same path; how dear to him must be that silent flood with its elm-trees, and great rolling hills; and how in times of darkness and discouragement he must have come to it for strength and consolation. The beauty of a river depends very much on its clearness and purity. The Rhine and the Tiber are more famous than the Merrimac; but their water is muddy and undrinkable.

Indeed the current of Whittier's life might not improperly be compared to the river beside which he dwelt so long. Commencing in the pure mountain air of the social and religious seclusion of his sect, the difficulties and limitations, which in his case waited upon the acquisition of knowledge, may well be compared to the passage through a rocky and unfruitful region, leaping as it were from one granite boulder to another; then no sooner has he gained depth and fulness from contact with natures like his own than he is caught in the mill-wheels of a great political revolution, he enters ardently into the anti-slavery conflict—as he says of himself in the "Tent on the Beach,"

"And one there was a dreamer born,
Who with a mission to fulfill
Had left the muses' haunts to turn
The crank of an opinion mill"—

and finally having escaped past all expectation from this turmoil, victorious and laurel-crowned, he goes calmly and steadily forward to the end. What makes this parallel rather surprising in its perfection is that Concord River empties itself into the Merrimac, and one might fancy that its waters carried Emerson's magnetic thought and influence to Whittier's own door. May not the career of any great man be compared to the course of a river? and especially the lives of our American poets would seem to resemble in their purity and transparency the rivers of New England.

Whittier's house, however, does not stand by the river's brim, but near the centre of the village, almost a mile away. It was a modest looking structure, in appearance much like the Alcott house at Concord, but not nearly so well situated. It faces towards the north, and has little land about it, though there is a vegetable-garden in the rear. Neither is there any protection for it from the cold blasts of winter. Here he lived, at first with his sister and after her death with his niece, Miss Lizzie Whittier, and I believe with another niece, who married a Mr. Caldwell; but also a large portion of the time quite alone, except for one or two servants, reading, meditating and writing poetry. A man who has that kind of work to do, can never be very lonely. The interior of the house, was plainly and comfortably furnished, and contained some fine pictures and handsome books, the gifts of Boston friends; but its chief ornament was the quiet dignity and amiable courtesy of the poet himself.

The eastern coast of New England is famous for its thunder-storms, and in the summer of 1872 there was one in the midst of nearly every afternoon. A number of persons were killed by the lightning that season, and Whittier also met with a narrow escape. It was one of the last days of June, and from our piazza we could see the masses of black cloud rolling down the Merrimac Valley, not thinking of the imminent peril, which they were bringing to our poet. At the same time Miss Lizzie Whittier and a lady friend were seated in the room on the right hand of the front-door, when crash! an electric bolt came through the wall like a rifle-shot, just above her friend's head, laying her out upon the floor, shivering a mirror into splinters; then went through the doorway and meeting John G. Whittier in the front hall, knocked him senseless, and seizing two slats from a blind it escaped through an open window into the garden. Miss Lizzie was the first to regain her feet, and her anxiety and terror, when she saw her uncle lying senseless on the floor, may readily be surmised. It proved, however, that none of them were seriously injured, though their heads were confused and unserviceable for several days, and they did not wholly recover from the effects of this *coup d' eclair* until after an excursion to the Isles of Shoals.

When Whittier was asked how the stroke felt, he said, "It was like a blow from a pile-driver,—and I would not like to have it repeated." The hole which the lightning made in the side of the house, could scarcely be distinguished from that of a large rifle bullet. A few days afterwards I saw a small house set on fire by the lightning, and it was consumed in a very few minutes, so one may infer how narrowly the Whittier family escaped a double danger.

He was a tall, and rather slender man, measuring almost exactly six feet, with sloping shoulders, and he stood so straight, as almost to be the personification of uprightness. No soldier was ever more erect, and this without the least stiffness or conventionality. His head was not large at the base, but high-crowned and finely arched. His eyes were magnificent, and can only be compared to Hawthorne's eyes, though not so clear. Marshal von Moltke had eyes like two brilliant lights; even the Emperor dared not look into them. Whittier's were not like this, but seemed to be lighted by hidden fires; very large, dark, and powerful. He had a sensitive and refined mouth, which was closed, as if by an effort of the will. In general appearance he resembled men of the Revolutionary period, as if a cotemporary of Washington had luckily been dropped out of the eighteenth century. He looked like Copley's portrait of Samuel Adams, but with a more intellectual, and less stubborn expression. From boyhood he was always fragile and ailing, could not sleep well at night, and would repeat poetry to himself (for he knew any quantity of it, without making an effort to memorize it) until he fell asleep again: yet to what an age he lived, and how much work he accomplished!

I am tempted here to quote from an essay by David A. Wasson, written nearly thirty years ago:—

"God gave Whittier a deep, hot, simple, strenuous and yet ripe and spherical, nature, whose twin necessities were, first that it *must* lay an intense grasp upon the elements of its experience, and, secondly, that it *must* work these up into some form of melodious completeness. History and the world gave him Quakerism, America, and Rural Solitude; and through this solitude went winding the sweet, old Merrimac Stream, the river that we would not wish to forget, even by the waters of the river of life! And it is into these elements that his genius, with its peculiar vital simplicity and intensity, strikes root. Historic reality, the great *facts* of his time, are the soil in which he grows, as they are with all natures of depth and energy." "We did not wish," said Goethe, "to learn, but to live."

The anti-slavery movement originated with the Quakers. It seems to have been their mission in America. Benjamin Lundy was a Quaker: Garrison and his friends were non-resistants, which is political Quakerism. Whittier was one of the first to join them, and none of them afterwards, except Wendell Phillips, had such influence with the public. Neither was he content with writing poetry for the cause, controversial lyrics and war-songs of freedom, but he took a lively interest in the affairs of the New England Society, went to its meetings and served on committees. Phillips said that once, when the socialistic element in the movement was threatening to come to open rupture with the more moderate Garrisonian party, Whittier by his tact and good sense, and a few timely remarks, did more than any other to harmonize matters, and prevent a dissolution. When Emerson was informed of this, he remarked, "I have always held Mr. Whittier in great respect; but this is the finest flower in the poet's wreath."

It is astonishing enough now to reflect what the early abolitionists attempted to do, and the manner in which they expected to do it. The empire of Christianity, and of true civilization, was to be established here in America for the first time and finally; the slaves were to be emancipated, intemperance prevented, and all warfare ended. This was to happen in a world where the Malthusian theory of population is a dominant reality, where millions are fighting every day for the bread of life, and thousands are dying from the lack of proper food, raiment and shelter. One of their number whose name will not appear in history, published a book, entitled "True Civilization an Immediate Necessity." Surely enough true civilization is and always has been an immediate necessity: a necessity like the feast of Tantalus: but how is it to be realized? The purest saints and noblest statesmen have struggled and died in despair in the attempt to elevate humanity a single inch above the condition in which they found it.

Of course such a chimera as that of the abolitionists could only be entertained by young, inexperienced and slightly educated men. Their effort was a noble one, a blunder in the right direction; but they had no conception of the explosive material which was contained in the doctrine of non-resistance. Instead of moral persuasion and an era of peace, there followed a desolating war in itself worse than fifty years of African Slavery. The abolitionists were blamed for that calamity very much as the Protestants have been blamed for the Massacre of St. Bartholomew; and yet without doubt they were responsible for a portion of it. Gunpowder cannot be made of sulphur and carbon alone, but saltpetre also must be added.

Those who remain in this immature condition of fixed ideas throughout life, purchase their experience at too high a rate. Whittier's poetic art saved him from this and separated him finally from his Garrisonian allies. With Garrison himself he always remained the best of friends; but after the Kansas troubles began he did not continue to look upon him as a leader, and in 1872 they were in political antagonism, Whittier endorsing Sumner, and Garrison supporting Grant.

Perhaps the writing of "Ichabod" and Webster's subsequent death gave an indication to Whittier of deeper life currents than he had known before; for about that time, it seems to have dawned on him that didactic poetry was not after all the best kind of poetry, and a work of art to be pure and holy, must exist for its own sake, and be justified by its own excellence. He refers to this intellectual change, not only in the lines already quoted, but in a sort of confession, written at an earlier period. He says—

"Art's perfect forms no moral need,
And beauty is its own excuse,"

and regrets that the highest reward of merit will never come to him on this account. He realizes now that he belongs to a party and has been looking at the world from the stand-point of party interest. In devoting himself more closely to his vocation as a poet he acquired that moral repose and better mental balance with which alone it is possible to see things as they are. From this time forward the quality of his verses shows a steady improvement.

The man possessed a deep nature and true breadth of character in spite of the limitations of his environment; yet there were certain prejudices and antipathies that adhered to him still. His unwillingness to listen to music, is rather to be attributed to the old quaker, puritanical notion that all sensuous enjoyment is sinful, than to the well known indifference of poets, for that sister art to which they owe so much. He once went so far as to take an interest in some musical glasses, and seemed to be pleased with the simple tunes that were played on them; but pianos and violins he had no liking for.

He enjoyed looking at portraits of distinguished men, but did not approve of religious pictures. Bayard Taylor presented him with a copy of his translation of "Faust," and he read it, for the sake of old acquaintance, but he did not like it and wondered especially what explanation "Goethe's apologists could make for the strange, and extraordinary characters in the second part." When some one asked him why he did not make a trip to

Europe he said: "Travelling does not seem to agree with me; but beside that, I do not think I should find pleasure in it. Their great cathedrals which people go to see, would not be of any account to me; and I am afraid I should not enjoy the works of art. I should like to see Switzerland; but there are also fine mountains over there"—pointing to New Hampshire.

His prohibitory friends alleged that he was a good deal disturbed by the five kinds of wine provided for the seventieth birth-day dinner, with which his Boston publishers honored him. He endeavored to escape from this dinner, and Messrs. Osgood and Company were obliged to send for him three times, and most urgently, before he could be persuaded to come. It is doubtful however if he objected to people's drinking wine in their own homes. [Footnote: To a friend, who sent him on his seventy-fifth birth-day a bottle of rare old Andalusian "Olovosa" with a bouquet of flowers, he wrote:—

"I hasten to thank thee, dear Mrs. — —, for thy kind note, and accompanying flowers, wreathing like Hafiz on Omar Khayyam's roses, the wine—not of Shiraz, but of storied Andalusia.

"I am not accustomed to tarry long at the wine—in this case I shall remember Paul's advice to Timothy.

"I am gratefully thy old friend,

"JOHN G. WHITTIER.

"Boston, Dec. 17, 1892."]

He is the only American poet who may be fairly said to have earned his living by his poems, though Longfellow might have done so, if it had been his fortune to reside in a country town. Whittier may have assisted sometimes in editing the local newspaper, and he once published a volume of rather tame prose-studies of the Shakers and other strange people who are found in the southern counties of New Hampshire. I never met with but one copy of it, and it could not have had a large circulation. He was not so much an observer of life and manners, as an imaginative thinker,—one whose reflections took the shape of ideal pictures. This, as Shakespeare would have called it, is the right complexion of the lyric poet.

His exchequer suffered however in the earlier part of his career on account of his principles. All the anti-slavery people suffered for their convictions in one way or another—just as the slave-holders suffered for theirs, in the end. Garrison was mobbed: Phillips, who might have amassed wealth, like Phocian, died in poverty: Sumner was murderously assaulted: John Brown, lost his life; and George L. Stearns, died of unresting toil during the war, and wrecked his fortune: but Whittier represented the heart of the American people, and after the publication of "Barbara Frietchie" the tide turned in his favor. "Snow-bound" had an extensive sale, and brought him in nearly ten-thousand dollars. "The Tent on the Beach" paid almost as well; and his collection of English and American poetry was a fortunate hit, on the part of his publishers, which Whittier's modest nature would not otherwise have thought of; so that he was well provided for, in old age, and could even have made a journey around the world like General Grant, if he had been so disposed.

His popularity soon attracted the attention of politicians who hoped to make use of it for the good of the country. He was too influential a member of the community to be overlooked. Senator Wilson, Speaker Colfax, Governor Claflin and others called upon him, congratulated him on the fortunate turn of affairs, and hoped they might be of service to him. Quakers have always had a good reputation for shrewdness, and Whittier was not lacking in that quality. He understood perfectly well what they wanted of him, and was a good deal amused by it, but he liked to converse with vigorous and experienced men, and could obtain from them a better understanding of affairs than was to be found in the newspaper. His letters on politics were always able and interesting; and he sometimes adopted exactly the opposite view from what his advisors would have liked to have him. It is true he formerly dedicated a poem to Colfax as an ideal statesman, but perhaps Whittier was more nearly right in this than public opinion has been, since that time.

He disliked being lionized and was rarely seen in public. The adoration of young women was of all things the most disagreeable to him. He created quite a sensation by appearing at one of Emerson's noon-day lectures in May, 1866, and as soon as the discourse was over he became the centre of a small circle of celebrities. Yet he seemed even more glad to meet his humbler and more familiar friends. He said, "If I come again, it will be to hear that man," referring to Wendell Phillips, who stood a little at one side watching Emerson and Whittier with the air of an art critic.

He said of the Boston Radical Club (which nevertheless contained the best intellectual life of its time) that he feared the saints went there not only to worship but to be worshipped:—a large part of the audience consisting of pretty young women. Yet he finally went there himself, for the sake of an interview with the most distinguished of his admirers, the Emperor of Brazil. This magnificent monarch, who may even be called the Marcus Aurelius of modern times, openly declared that there was nothing in North America that he wished so much to see as the poet Whittier. A meeting was accordingly arranged, and no sooner had Dom Pedro caught sight of Whittier (whom he recognized from the pictures he possessed) than he hastened to embrace him, and would certainly have kissed the astonished Quaker, after the fashion that prevails among the Latin races, if Whittier had permitted him the least opportunity. After paying his compliments in a handsome manner to the assembled company the Emperor took his leave again, and insisted on carrying off the poet with him. One might like to know what sort of a conversation two such different and almost antipodal friends had together for that one hour in a lifetime.

The climate of the Isles of Shoals exactly suited Whittier's dreamy nature. He would wander from the piazza into the billiard-room, and back again to the piazza, and then look at the sea for an hour or more without speaking a word to any one. Indeed he talked very little even with those who knew him best, and strangers had no chance at all with him. There was something respectful in the hush of conversation whenever he approached a group of people who were talking loudly or laughing. I never met him walking over the rocks, or knew of his going out on the water either for sailing or fishing. One foggy evening when some of us were playing a game of writing verses in the hotel parlor, one of the ladies seeing Whittier alone, in a corner of the room, boldly invited him to join us, which he did with a very pleasant alacrity. It was noticed however that his compositions were not any better or even so good as those of the others, and we suspected that he took pains not to excel the rest of the company.

Yet he could talk in a vigorous manner when the right occasion presented itself. There was a certain Colonel Greene who frequented Appledore in those years: a high-minded socialistic thinker, who had resigned a commission in the United States Army, during the war with the Florida Indians, on account of the government's breach of faith with Osceola. He was a born controversialist and always ready to discuss any subject in politics, religion or philosophy. John Weiss was not far behind him in this line, and delighted to set him going for the benefit of those who liked to hear. No sea air was sufficiently narcotic to dull the edge of Colonel Greene's argument. When these two were once discussing a book on pantheism, which had lately been published by Rev. J. W. Manning of the Old South Church, Whittier, who had been walking to and fro on the piazza just within reach of their voices, finally, came up and said: "I told Manning that the one kind of pantheist he had omitted from his book, was the orthodox pantheist. For that matter, I believe there are pantheists in every religious sect. They start like Professor Parsons the Swedenborgian, with the proposition that as even God could not make the universe out of nothing, he must have made it out of Himself; and you cannot argue them away from it. At the same time, they will insist that they are perfectly good Christians." He then cited several instances of this which had come under his own observation: and Colonel Greene also remembered some cases; but this was the only time we knew Whittier to speak on a religious question.

Longfellow, Tennyson and Whittier were the three most popular poets of the latter part of the present century, and it is difficult to determine which of them may be considered the best. While neither of them rises to the very highest rank, each has excellences peculiarly his own. Whittier does not equal the others in their graceful diction and rare metrical skill, but he surpasses them in earnestness and intensity. He paints in deeper colors, and with a firmer touch. The longer and more ambitious poems of Tennyson and Longfellow are interesting, but they lack the strength, vigor and greatness of design which are inseparable from all the noblest works of art.

They are written to please, rather than to educate the human race. Their shorter pieces are the best ones. Whittier's chief excellence is to be found in his ballads; in the "Wreck at Rivermouth," "Skipper Ireson," "The Relief of Lucknow," "Barbara Frietchie" and others. Nothing is more rare than a fine ballad. Coleridge's ballad of the "Ancient Mariner" is probably the greatest English poem written since Milton's time, and there are many old English ballads which are nearly equal to it. The ballad of "Mary Garvin," simply as a work of art, takes the first place among Longfellow's poems. Tennyson and Whittier both tried their hands on the siege of Lucknow, and Whittier carried off the prize.

His verses are always sensible, healthy and elevating. Complaint has been made that they are too much haunted by the spectre of his schoolmate; but without saying this, we could wish that such an immature affection had been replaced afterwards by a deeper and more manly attachment. He was assisted in the arrangement of his collection of poetry (which Lowell and other good critics considered the best we have) by his poetical friend Miss Lucy Larcom, and this was chiefly no doubt that she might receive a share of the profits from its publication. The sonnets from Shakespeare and many others, were of her selection. The art of poetry came so naturally to Whittier, that he said he could not understand why every one did not write it as well as or better than he could.

At the time of Hawthorne's last visit to the Isles of Shoals in company with his friend the ex-President, there was also a party of business men from Concord, New Hampshire, who tried to make his acquaintance, but without much success. Afterwards we went to Portsmouth with the same party and were becalmed on the way for nearly four hours, so that we had an excellent chance to become acquainted with our fellow passengers. One of them said:—"Nathaniel Hawthorne was a very reserved man. There's Franklin Pierce: he has been President of the United States, and yet anyone can go up and speak to him; but we found Hawthorne very different." Of course we had to tell this on our return, and Whittier laughed heartily. Mrs. Thaxter said, "Reserved was no word for it;" and Whittier added, "Hawthorne was a strange puzzle. I never felt quite sure whether I knew him or not. He never seemed to be doing anything, and yet he did not like to be disturbed at it." He disliked to hear people say that Hawthorne wrote the life of General Pierce for the sake of a government office. They were old college friends, and without doubt he would have obtained the office whether he wrote it or not. If he wished to live in Italy Buchanan should have given him the consulship of Leghorn or Venice. He looked on "Septimus Felton" as a failure, and thought that probably Hawthorne considered it so himself. He thought it not unlikely that Hawthorne would outlive every other writer of his time.

At another time he came to me and said, "What deep problems of government are you thinking over there all by yourself?" I laughed and told him that I was thinking of Rome; and how much that little patch of water looked like the piece of sea in Guido's Aurora; but I was glad to have him speak of politics, for the present condition of affairs was such as to give every serious man anxiety for the moral welfare of the country.

"Indeed it is," he replied. "What we read in the newspapers is bad enough; but I have information from private sources which represents matters as being even worse than is generally supposed." [Footnote: This was in 1875.]

"Perhaps," I said, "it is one of those evils which will cure itself after a certain time."

"It will, no doubt," he answered, "bring about a strong reaction against the Republican party; but even that is a thing to be deplored. Meanwhile what an example we present to the monarchical governments of Europe!"

"I suppose," said I, "that it is one of the consequences of our civil war."

"Yes," said he, "I am ready to agree to that,—a long and protracted war must have a hardening and brutalizing influence on the community even when it is fought for a good cause."

"Did not Hawthorne," I said, "predict something like this in an article in the 'Atlantic Monthly'?"

"Yes," he replied, "I remember that article,—it was just a year before his death,—and there was a good deal of wisdom in it. Some of my friends are inclined to think that woman suffrage would improve the present condition of politics, but I do not feel sure that it would."

"I have no doubt it would do good if only the sensible women were permitted to vote," I said. "My faith is that what we need to purify politics in America is not an extension, but a restriction of the suffrage. It is easy to see, for instance, how favorably that would work in the city of New York, which with its custom-house is now the heaviest burden we have to bear."

What Whittier thought of this idea I never knew; he seemed to be reflecting on it when the ladies of his party came in sight and we both rose to meet them.

Though he was not fond of travelling, he liked to read books of travel; and once, according to his doctor's advice, spent a winter at Amesbury reading everything of the kind that he could hear of and obtain. He spoke of Wilson's book on the Himalaya Mountains as the most interesting of them. "It seems as if there was nothing that a cultivated Englishman could not and would not go through with," he said. I mentioned Humboldt. "Yes," he replied, "Humboldt certainly accomplished wonderful things, but the Germans are generally more cautious and prudent. A cultivated Englishman seems to be equal to anything." Among modern travellers however, Vambery, the Hungarian, takes the highest rank.

At a later period, I was journeying through the White Mountains and reached West Ossipee one afternoon tired with travelling and weary from a sleepless night. I hastened to my room and threw myself upon the bed, but had scarcely closed my eyes when there was a knock at the door and there stood Mr. Whittier,—the pleasantest of all apparitions for some years. The next few days were like dwelling in the islands of the blest, compared with the ordinary current of human life. It was a holiday within a holiday. He was surrounded by charming ladies, among them his niece Mrs. Caldwell, and as it was late in the season we had the Bear Camp House—a place that now ought to be historic—almost to ourselves.

We had never known Whittier to be so friendly and companionable before. We walked under the elms, talked about books, and our absent friends, gazed at the mountains, and admired the sunsets which just at that time were remarkably brilliant. There was one, I remember, composed largely of luminous clouds, and a general translucent effect of the atmosphere, which Whittier could not remember he had ever seen the like of. He said, "I don't believe Emerson loves Nature any better than I do, though he has written more about it." There was a delightful lady in the party who told us pleasant and amusing stories of New York social life. She could go on in this way for a very good length of time, and Whittier would listen to her without saying a word, exactly as if she were reading to him.

The magnates of West Ossipee had named a mountain near Chocorua for Whittier and challenged him to climb to the top of it and christen it properly with a bottle of champagne, but he said No, that his days for climbing were over; that he thought mountains belonged to the whole country and he had no desire to appropriate any of them. He liked such names as Chocorua, Katahdin and Wachusett much better for mountains than Washington and Adams. The Bear Camp House is a rare sort of a tasteful country inn, and its proprietor was of course very proud of his distinguished guest, but at the same time sufficiently dignified to prevent this from being too apparent. It was there Whittier spent the last summers of his life, as long as he was able to leave his own home.

In his old age he enjoyed the celebrity of his more vigorous years as if it had been the fame of a constant friend; but I think he enjoyed still more the consciousness of having succeeded in living through life as he intended to do in the beginning.